Faith Matters
The Ebb and Flow of Unstoppable Hope

Greg Asimakoupoulos

On the Tracks Media

Faith Matters: The Ebb and Flow of Unstoppable Hope
Copyright © 2024 by Greg Asimakoupoulos

All rights reserved. No part of this book may be reproduced or transmitted in any form or by any means, electronic or mechanical, including photocopying, recording, or any information storage and retrieval system, except in the case of brief passages embodied in critical reviews or articles, without permission from the author:
Asimakoupoulos@gmail.com

Printed in the United States of America.
ISBN: 979-8-9869449-4-4

Cover and Interior Design: Rick Lindholtz for On the Tracks Media

On the Tracks Media
rlindholtz@icloud.com

10   9   8   7   6   5   4   3   2   1

Endorsements

Greg Asimakoupoulos is a poet, prophet and pastor. My father-in-law enjoyed getting to know him as a ministry colleague and I am, too. Greg's book will stretch your faith and fire your imagination.

Mark Batterson
New York Times bestselling author of *The Circle Maker*, *Chase the Lion* and *Win the Day*

"At its core, *Faith Matters* is a book of wisdom. In some ways it's like a modern day *Book of Proverbs*, offering up a wonderful 'chowder' of engaging stories that deliver inspiring insights and solid principles to live by, from a man who has spent his life in faithful ministry. This is a book to be savored in small bites as a morning devotion or a bedtime snack. Keep a copy by your favorite chair or on your bedroom nightstand and enjoy."

Rich Stearns, President Emeritus of World Vision US and author of *The Hole in Our Gospel* and *Lead Like It Matters To God*.

In Faith Matters, Greg Asimakoupoulos has given us a collection of personal vignettes that invite the reflections on life's rhythms we claim we want. I have known Greg for years and am always amazed at his ease in chasing hunches and ideas. He presents them with an unassuming clarity that encourages our quests and hopes. He connects dots that most people would not realize need connecting. Further, these observations are set in the context of relationships. I don't know anyone who has more connections in more places than Greg! Therein is the wonder of the ebb and flow of unstoppable hope that makes his thoughts so relevant.

J. Craig Thorpe, Northwest artist and speaker
and a former Presbyterian minister

Faith Matters may be my favorite book by Greg Asimakoupoulos…a man of faith who beautifully describes snapshots of life that most of us would miss. For instance, he notices the dash between the dates on James Dean's gravestone… the Hollywood heart throb who died at 24. Have any of us wondered about that dash between our own DOB and DOD? Greg does. Or consider the peer pressure of a high school senior in a courtroom witnessing his father reverting the family name from Smith… which everyone can pronounce… to their true name, Asimakoupoulos, and why that was one of the two most important dates in his dad's life? (The book kindly provides a pronunciation guide.)

SQuire Rushnell, author, The Godwink books & movies

Dr. Deana Porterfield

Table of **Contents**

The Dash of Life	1
Born-Again Again	4
The Olympics of Life	7
An Unforgettable Olympic Moment	10
Practicing What I've Preached	13
Never Underestimate the Power of the Past	16
Returning an Overdue Book	19
A Blueprint for Success	22
Lessons from "The Boys in the Boat"	25
The Impressions We Leave Behind	28
Faces in the Forest	31
A Tribute to a Timeless Carroll	34
More Than a Christmas Card	37
Let's Talk About Angels	40
Redemption: A Case Study	43
The Unsent Christmas Card	46
What if Jesus Had Never Been Born?	48
The Difference a Day Makes	51
My Best Friend Billy	54
Eternal Love: A Valentine Story	57
A Prayer for Unity in the Spirit of Dr. Seuss	60
Love is a Verb	62
A Day for Patrick and Other Saints	65
Brotherly Love and Sister Cities	68
An Easter Godwink in Switzerland	71
Easter Sunday (Take 2)	74

A Somber Anniversary	77
An Invitation to Number Our Days	80
Learning to Say Learning to Say *Grüezi*	83
In the Shadow of the Mountain	86
Oh, The People You Will Meet	89
God is Now Here	92
Finding Common Ground	95
Being Alert to the World Around You	98
Reflections on a Fifty-Year Reunion	101
Oh, the Places You'll Go	104
An Invitation to Live Like Jesus	107
I Lift Up My Eyes to the Hills	110
There is More to Life than Baseball	113
The Her Behind the Hymn	116
Rejection is Not Final!	119
Reflecting on a Somber Anniversary	121
Let's Hear It for Leftovers	124
Remember, to Say Thanks	127
The Tragic Story Behind a Timeless Hymn	130
The Innkeeper Has a Name	133
Looking for Aslan in Everyday Life	136
A Tribute to a Maestro	139
The Tale of the Returned Letter	142
A Different Kind of Rock Collection	145
What I Learned from Playing Barbies	148
Let's Hear it for Mentors!	151
Two Men, Six Degrees and a B-52	154

No Ordinary Anniversary	157
In Praise of a Family Tree	160
It's a Wonderful Place	163
An Antidote to Disenchantment with Church	166
A Photograph Memory with Spiritual Implications	169
Lessons from the Resurrection Tree	172
A Ray of Hope	175
Life is Like a Waiting Room	179
Be Alert to the Beauty Around Us	182
Ports-of-Call on an Unforgettable Cruise	185
Afternoon Tea with the Galloping Gourmet	188
Lessons from an Alaska Glacier	191
Loving Like Jesus	194
A Father's Day Reflections	197
Playing Church was More Than Just Play	199
Words to the Wise!	202
A Tale of Two Elsies	205
A Preview of Coming Attractions	207
Minding Your 'p's and 'q's	209
Poetry is My Bag	212
A Mane Metaphor for the Almighty	214
By the Dawn's Early Light	216
Graceland or Grazeland	219
Prayer: A Capitol Idea	222
Celebrating the Oscars in Our Lives	224
A Time for Jesus	227
Hail to the Chiefs	230

Memories of a Sad Day and an Unforgettable Poem 233
A Godwink in the Garbage 236
Forget Looking for Shadows, Look in the Mirror 238
A Celebration of a Fifty Year Friendship 241
They Had a Dream! What's Yours? 244
We Don't Talk About… 246
A Classic Movie with Timeless Message 249
In Search of Balance 252
Picturing Contentment: Life Lessons from the Original Facebook 255
There Actually is Crying in Baseball! 257
The Hunger in My Heart 260
An Invitation to Paint Rocks 263
Skookum, Santa and the Searching Eyes of God 266
No Vacation from Vocation 269
A Labor Day Weekend Reflection 272
Let's Hear it for Family Reunions 275
A Puff Felt Round the World 278
The Passion (Revisited) 281
Perspective is Everything 284
Welcome to Awe-tumn 287
Fully Rely on God 290
A Life-Saving Rescue Remembered 293
This is Holy Ground 296
A Tale of Three Amigos 299
Your House versus the White House 302
Preparing for the Trip of a Lifetime 305
Faith Matters! It Really Does 308

Foreword

Greg Asimakoupoulos loves words. He loves the swing and swirl of language, the way a well-crafted sentence can dance off the page and resonate in the heart.

How do we know?

Well, for starters, take a look at his last name: Asimakoupoulos. Eight vowels! You practically get a vocabulary lesson just trying to pronounce it. (Awesome-ah-COPE-ah-less). But we also know Greg loves words because he and his wife Wendy have been guests at our dining room table where we played Scrabble. You know, the word-game for word-nerds and logophiles who get way too excited about triple word scores. (As an aside, Greg told us he actually proposed to Wendy on a Scrabble board.)

Greg is the kind of guy who doesn't just play Scrabble, he relishes it, savoring each opportunity to use those obscure, high-scoring words that make the rest of us reach for the dictionary. In fact, we kid you not, he brought a dictionary with him. He claimed it was for "reference," but we all knew better. It was his secret weapon, his ace in the hole, his way of turning a casual game night into an intellectual battleground.

Greg doesn't just love words, he paints with them, using each phrase as a brushstroke to craft vivid landscapes of meaning and emotion. And in *Faith Matters: The Ebb and Flow of Unstoppable Hope*, his passion for language and his deep-seated faith come together like colors on a canvas, blending seamlessly to create a masterpiece that speaks to the heart and soul.

Faith indeed does matter. It serves as the bedrock upon which we build our lives, offering a sense of purpose and direction even when the path ahead is unclear. In a world that can often seem chaotic and unpredictable, faith provides an anchor, grounding us in something greater than ourselves. It reassures us that there is a meaning beyond the day-to-day struggles and that we are part of a larger story unfolding. Faith invites us to trust, even when the evidence isn't clear, and to believe in God's goodness, even when faced with adversity.

Hope, in many ways, is faith's closest companion. It's the light that breaks through the darkest clouds, the inner strength that fuels us when we feel like giving up. Hope is what keeps us moving forward, one step at a time, even when the odds seem insurmountable. Unstoppable hope empowers us to face life's challenges head-on. Together, faith and hope create a powerful synergy that equips us to navigate the ups and downs of life, reminding us that even in the ebb and flow, there is an unstoppable force of love and purpose guiding us forward.

It's this dynamic duo of faith and hope that Greg captures so beautifully in this book. He's got a knack, or maybe more of a trademark style in his wordsmithing. He looks creatively at the humdrum of daily existence and finds unexpected significance in the seemingly mundane. Through his beloved poetry and writings like this, Greg sees the threads of a larger narrative weaving through everyday life. He has a gift for taking what might appear ordinary and revealing the extraordinary within it.

And so, it's no surprise that Greg Asimakoupoulos, with his multi-syllabic-last name and his love of words, has crafted a book that feels like an enjoyable game of Scrabble. Each chapter is like a carefully chosen word, placed perfectly on the board of life, adding depth and meaning to the overall picture. Just as Greg finds joy in discovering those high-scoring words that surprise and delight, he finds profound insights in the everyday experiences that many might overlook.

Reading *Faith Matters* is like playing Scrabble with Greg: it's thoughtful, inspiring, and full of unexpected turns. And while you might not need a dictionary to read this book, you'll certainly find your heart and mind expanded, challenged, and ultimately uplifted. Greg's love for words is evident on every page, and his passion for faith and hope will leave you with a renewed appreciation for the beautiful complexity of life's unfolding story. After all, when Greg's at the table, whether it's Scrabble or life, you know you're in for something meaningful, memorable, and truly extraordinary.

Drs. Les & Leslie Parrott
#1 New York Times bestselling authors of
Saving Your Marriage Before It Starts

Introduction

After my mom died in 2019, I sorted through an expandable folder of my writings she'd saved. Among the newspaper and magazine articles in which she'd taken personal pride was a "letter to the editor" I'd written in 1970 while in high school. It dawned on me that my career as a published freelance writer began when I was eighteen. My passion for putting my thoughts in print began with an opinion piece about President Nixon's handling of the Vietnam war.

Since that time, I have written seventeen books, over three hundred articles for various periodicals (mostly religious) and countless columns for local newspapers. These papers include the Seattle Times, the Kitsap Sun, the Daily Herald, the Mercer Island Reporter and the Wenatchee World.

Faith Matters is a compilation of newspaper columns I've written over the past several years. It is a sequel to *Intersections*, a similar collection of published essays, that came out in 2022. The order in which these columns appear in this volume is random. Each piece is a stand-alone column that does not depend of what comes before or after it.

As you might guess, writing a regular newspaper column is a source of joy as well as an expression of my creativity. It all began a quarter century ago while living in suburban Chicago. The editor of the Daily Herald liked a freelance article I had submitted relating our family's fascination with a reality TV show called "Survivor" that had just debuted. In response I was invited to write a weekly "faith and values" piece on any topic I wanted.

When our family relocated from the Midwest to the Pacific Northwest five years later, I approached the editor of the Mercer Island Reporter. Once again, I was welcomed to contribute content on a regular basis.

What began as a monthly assignment morphed into twice a month. To my delight, the Wenatchee World (the newspaper I read growing up) reprinted my columns from time to time. And then, out of the blue, I was encouraged to submit a weekly article for the Sunday edition of my hometown paper.

My hope is that *Faith Matters* will encourage and inspire the reader to be alert for Godwinks their lives as well as recognizing just how much faith does matters in the everyday stuff of life. Upon closer examination there is ample evidence that hope is unstoppable even though (like the Snoqualmie River that flows near our home) at times it ebbs and flows.

Speaking of the Snoqualmie River, one of the most popular tourist attractions in the Seattle area is Snoqualmie Falls where the river cascades over a strata of ancient rock for 268 uninterrupted feet. My favorite photo of "Sno Falls" was taken by Don Detrick and is featured on a postcard. My favorite painting of "The Falls" is by my longtime friend J. Craig Thorpe and graces the cover of this book. I am grateful to Craig for allowing me the use of his image for this project.

Greg Asimakoupoulos

Dedication

This book is dedicated to Edwin and Star Asimakoupoulos (my parents) and Hugh and Norma Steven (my wife's parents). My mom and dad taught me how much faith matters from the time I was a toddler. My in-laws modeled for me the time and perseverance required to write and publish articles and books that convey Biblical truth. I am indebted to both sets of loving parents.

The Dash of Life

Walking is good for your health, and I believe that strolling through cemeteries helps one maintain a healthy perspective on life. Headstones can be a most effective means of calibrating one's attitude about what's really important this side of the grave.

While on a speaking engagement in central Indiana some years back, I made an intentional detour off Interstate 69 to get to the little town of Fairmount. That's where Jim Davis, the creator of the Garfield comic strip, grew up. It is better known, however, as the hometown of Hollywood legend James Dean. Fairmount is where the perpetual 24-year-old is buried. He was born Feb. 8, 1931, and died Sept. 30, 1955.

Since I was only 3 years old when this '50s heartthrob died, I have not been overly preoccupied with his life. But after watching a television documentary on James Dean, I'd become intrigued with his cult-like following. Since I was traveling so close to where he grew up and was buried, I decided to take some time and check out Fairmount. I wanted to walk around the sleepy Midwest town and soak in some of the ambiance that contributed to the life of the person that millions still praise long after his death.

A grocery checkout clerk gave me directions to the home of one of Dean's high school friends. When I stated the purpose of my spontaneous visit, Bob Pulley invited me into his farmhouse on the edge of town.

Bob had a lot of memories of Dean. He pulled out his 1949 high school yearbook and showed me photographs of the two of them in a school play and on the track team. He smiled as he recounted their senior trip to Washington, D.C. For Bob, it was as if it were only a few years ago.

I asked him about his last visit with his famous friend. Dean had returned home for a photo shoot a few months before his untimely death. According to Bob, he was still the same old "Jimmy." He told me about the funeral. He had been one of the pallbearers.

I drove to the Fairmount cemetery and stood in front of Dean's grave. Fresh flowers graced his final resting place. Photographs and cigarettes were strewn at the foot of his headstone. Fans had left them there to commemorate the late actor's birthday.

As I stared at the grave marker, I was impressed by its simplicity. James B. Dean 1931 – 1955. How quickly his life was over. I looked to the left of his grave to see his father and stepmother's marker. I looked to the right to see the marker of the uncle and aunt who raised him after his mother died when he was only nine.

Although the names and dates were different, each gravestone had something in common: between the birth date and death date, each had a small dash.

The dash represents a person's life, with all the happiness and heartache that come our way. It stands for the failures and successes we achieve. It stands for what we do with the opportunities God gives us.

The fact that it is a dash is most appropriate. Whether we live 24 years or 94, our lives speed by like the time it takes to run a 100-yard dash.

Next time you take a walk through your local cemetery, look at the names. Look at the dates. Consider the dashes.

As you do, think about this: We can't control the date we're born. We can't control the date we die. But we can decide what we will do with our dash. To that end, determine to make the most of your dash as you re-evaluate your purpose in the world. Don't take it for granted. Resist the temptation to run away from the reality of what's to come. Don't be a rebel without a cause.

Consider what a first-century Christian leader in the Roman Empire wrote, "Live life then, with a due sense of responsibility, not as men who do not know the meaning of life, but as those who do. Make the best use of your time?" (Ephesians 5:15)

Born-Again Again

I was "born again" as a boy when I confessed Christ as my personal Savior. When I turned seventeen, I experienced a second rebirth. Fifty-five years ago this week, my identity changed forever.

August 13, 1969, was the day my parents Edwin and Star Smith of Wenatchee stood with me and my brother Marc before a Chelan County judge. As the sound of a gavel reverberated in the empty courtroom, the Smiths heard him declare that from that day forward they would be known as the Asimakoupoulos family.

After my paternal grandfather emigrated from Greece and became a naturalized U.S. citizen, he changed his name from Haralambos Athanasius Asimakoupoulos to Harry Kenneth Smith. Proud of his new country, my Papou chose the most typical American name he could imagine. He married Margaret Turley, an All-American young woman from the Blue Ridge Mountains of Virginia. Harry and Margaret Smith had six kids. The Smith Clan lived on the Clearwater River outside of Lewiston, Idaho.

When my dad married and had two sons of his own, his personal pride in his ethnic ancestry was camouflaged by his alias. After visiting Greece for the first time in 1960, Dad fell in love with his father's homeland. He regretted Grampa Smith's decision to abandon a name that called to mind his Greek heritage. On more than one occasion, he told my younger brother and me what our real name was. He hinted that he might like to take it back again. Repeatedly we encouraged him to reclaim a name that was authentically (and uniquely) ours.

Several weeks before my senior year at Wenatchee High School, my dad decided to act on his inclination. He made an appointment at the law office of local attorney Robert Connor. The legal application to change our name was initiated. A nervous excitement twisted in my gut.

Days went by as the endless paperwork was processed. And then on August 13, with the bang of the gavel, it was official. The Smiths were now the Asimakoupouloses. A month later as I sat in Mrs. Valaas' French class, I practiced my new signature wishing my grandfather (who died when I was only five) had lived to appreciate our decision.

After fifty-five years, I can honestly say I have never regretted the decision to change our name. In spite of all the hassles and headaches associated with such a major change, the resulting sense of pride more than made up for the inconvenience.

I took joy in knowing my dad's dream to reclaim his ancestral identity had been achieved. In years to come, I did my own dreaming, daydreaming about getting married and passing on that 14-letter surname to my sons.

I guess the Almighty has a sense of humor. When I eventually got married, my wife blessed me with three beautiful daughters (but no boys). To date, two of my three daughters have married and neither chose to hyphenate their maiden name with that of their husband. I doubt my unmarried daughter will keep her name when I one day walk her down the aisle. But at least my brother Marc has a son who can keep the reclaimed name alive.

Sixteen years ago, when my father's lengthy battle with prostate cancer was drawing to a close, he and I reminisced about two highlights that marked his 82 years of life. One occurred on September 2, 1945. The other on August 13, 1969. Both dates documented milestones that gave "the kid from Clearwater" a sense of personal pride.

Dad never quit talking about being aboard the USS Missouri at the surrender ceremony that marked the conclusion of World War II. (He was the Marine honor guard assigned to the general who signed the peace treaty for the Soviet Union). Dad also smiled as he recalled the day our family name was legally changed from Smith to Asimakoupoulos. Remembering both occasions, he was unabashedly patriotic. He had pride in the country from which his father had come and pride in the nation in which he was privileged to grow up.

Over the past five and a half decades, that big fat Greek name has served our family well. It has been a conversation starter as well as the means by which people are more apt to recall having met us. Once someone learns to pronounce it (awesome-ah-COPE-ah-less), they never forget it.

The Olympics of Life

Over the past two weeks we have been glued to our television sets watching the Olympics from the "city of light." There were memorable moments (like the opening ceremonies in the pelting rain) that we will recall for years to come. At least until our nation hosts the Summer Games in four years.

But we don't need to wait for the Los Angeles Olympics to participate in the "Olympics of Life." Regardless of whether you frequent a gym or exercise at home, here are some events that anyone can incorporate into their daily routines.

Remember to stretch. Flexibility is not as prevalent as it once was. In our current cultural environment, there is not much stretching to reach across the aisle on Capitol Hill (or in church). Differences in opinion and perspective are easily weaponized. There is a tendency to become rigid and unbending to the point of fracturing relationships within families and within congregations. What ever happened to the old adage *"In essentials unity, in non-essentials liberty, and in all things charity?"* In the Olympics of Life stretching is a prerequisite to reaching out in love.

Recognize the balance beam of work and play. One of the highlights of the Paris Games for me was watching Simone Biles and her teammates on the balance beam. They demonstrated with seeming ease and grace just how beautiful maintaining one's balance can be.

And whereas the fruit of a balanced life is a thing of beauty, such fruit is not we Americans are known for. While watching the Olympic coverage, I heard a commentator mention how the French work in order to live whereas most Americans live to work. An unbalanced approach to our vocations can find us making a living without experiencing a meaningful life.

Wrestle worries and hurdle over fear. Like pebbles in a runner's shoe, worry and fear keep us from maximizing our potential. We should learn from the Greco/Roman wrestlers and hurdlers we saw in Paris. They demonstrated how how to pin and leap over whom and what stood in their way. They faced their opponents and obstacles with the belief they can win. Faith in a God (who is bigger than whatever we are facing) can give us the same belief. There is a quote from Corrie ten Boom, a Holocaust survivor, that hangs on our refrigerator. It says, *Worrying doesn't empty tomorrow of its sorrow, it empties today of its strength.*

Swim upstream against the current of what's current. After Paris invested $1.5 billion into cleaning up the notoriously polluted Seine River, swimmers were prevented from participating in certain events for nearly a week. The pollution remained hazardous to the health of the athletes. Giving-in to cultural trends in order to be popular or to gain the approval of others can be just as toxic. As people of faith, we are called to take our cues from the truths of God's Word in an attempt to perform before an audience of One.

Dive into what needs to be done. Can you imagine standing on the diving platform there in Paris? It's comparable to standing atop a three-story building. As my Norwegian grandfather used to say, "uff-da!" But those Olympic divers have learned to leap with confidence. In the Olympics of Life, we are often called to jump into tasks that at times seem overwhelming. Procrastination is a nemesis we must resist. Like the paparazzi in Paris, what distracts us can take our minds off what needs doing. Delaying the inevitable only makes what we are called to do more difficult.

Walk with God. Are you familiar with that Olympic event where the walkers rapidly waddle around the track? To the uninitiated, the participants in that event look funny. But those are serious athletes. The first race-walking competition was held at the 1908 Games in London. In the Olympics of Life, the kind of walking I have in mind requires frequency and not speed. Walking with God is a daily activity in which we enjoy communion and conversation with the Creator of the universe. It's an exercise regimen that helps us remain spiritually fit. And like those in Alcoholics Anonymous have discovered, progress is made one step at a time.

An Unforgettable Olympic Moment

A few months before my wife and I became engaged, we saw a movie that we knew nothing about. As we left the theater that summer night in 1981, we were speechless. The acting, the soundtrack and the message of *Chariots of Fire* deeply impacted both Wendy and me. I wanted to know more about Eric Liddell whose life as an Olympic athlete and a man of faith had been portrayed on the big screen.

In the film about his life, I loved how Eric responded to his sister when she challenged his desire to race instead of being involved in the family's missionary pursuits. *"Jenny, God made me for a purpose... But He also made me fast. And when I run, I feel His pleasure."*

Who was this Scottish runner who won the right to compete in the 1924 Paris Olympics but, upon learning that his event would take place on a Sunday, refused to run? What are we make of his personal conviction to not compete on the Lord's Day? And then, what became of this young man who actually won first place when allowed to compete in another event on a different day?

Over time I would learn that the Flying Scotsman (after his gold medal performance in the 400 meters) eventually joined his family in China working for the London Missionary Society. Following the Japanese invasion of China and the outbreak of World War 2, Eric became of prisoner of war where he used his spiritual knowledge and athletic prowess to encourage his fellow prisoners. Tragically, Eric died of a brain tumor just a few months before liberation.

One scene I particularly recall from the film is that of Eric standing behind the pulpit in an English-speaking church in Paris giving the sermon on the Sunday he was originally scheduled to compete. That scene came to mind a couple months ago when Wendy and I were spending a weekend in Paris before returning home from a three-month ministry assignment in Switzerland. As we worshipped at the American Church in Paris, I wondered if that gothic cathedral with Tiffany stained-glass windows was the church portrayed in *Chariots of Fire*.

Following the worship service, I asked the pastor if this was *the* church. He told me it couldn't have been since ACP was constructed three years after the Paris Games of 1924. I later discovered that there was another English-speaking church in Paris where Eric was the guest preacher. All the same, it was special to attend church in Paris on the one-hundredth anniversary of Eric Liddell's performance on the track and in the pulpit.

While I am impressed by the courage and personal conviction displayed by Eric in choosing not to compete on a Sunday, I am wondering if I would have made the same choice. In all honesty, I don't think I would have. Although raised in a decade where Sunday blue laws were still enforced, I have come to interpret keeping the Sabbath holy in a less-legalistic way. While I attend church most every Sunday, I am not opposed to going to a Mariners game or watching the Seahawks in a sports bar. I have been known to run to Safeway for a quart of milk or a frozen pizza.

On the other hand, I have Jewish neighbors who strictly honor the Sabbath by not working, driving or attending sporting events. They do not watch television or use the internet. I respect them for their discipline. I am impressed by their willingness to walk to and from the synagogue in all kinds of weather. My neighbors are willing to sacrifice convenience or risked being misunderstood in order to practice their faith.

As we watch the athletes from around the globe compete over the next couple weeks, we will see the fruit of self-discipline and personal conviction. Those who represent their home country in Paris are there because they made difficult choices to live out their dream in spite of the cost.

For Eric Liddell, honoring the Lord's Day (as he understood it) was a tangible way of feeling God's pleasure in addition to running. Perhaps we need to ask what the non-negotiables are for us when it comes to pursuing our dreams all the while practicing our faith.

Practicing What I've Preached

Seventeen years ago I had the privilege of officiating the wedding of Coach Mike Holmgren's youngest daughter. It was the natural culmination of a fifteen-year friendship with the Holmgren family.

Mike and his wife Kathy became personal friends when I was a pastor in Northern California. Shortly after he left the Forty-Niners organization to become head coach of the Green Bay Packers, our family moved to Illinois. My allegiance to the leader of The Pack in the heart of Bears Country found me cheering for the Packers. I was definitely in the minority on Sunday afternoons. As a result, I wore my Cheesehead discreetly.

After a handful of years and two Super Bowl appearances, Mike moved to Seattle to become head coach of the Seahawks. And in 2005 when I accepted a call to a church in suburban Seattle, I became the head coach's lead pastor. And as you might expect, I also became a devoted 12. Amazingly, within a few months of our move to Washington State, I was cheering for Mike and the Hawks in Super Bowl XL.

When Mike's daughter approached me about coaching her and her fiancé through their premarital counseling, I was delighted. We huddled at our local Starbucks to review the plays I've discovered lead to a committed relationship. Over lattes, we planned their ceremony.

As the big day drew near, I pictured the Xs and Os that inevitably were going through Coach Mike's head. I wanted to share something with my friend that would be meaningful. Because I had never been the father of the bride at that point, I could only imagine the emotions that were crowding his heart. Putting pen to paper, I came up with the following:

When you stand beside your daughter
and you hear the Wedding March,
I am guessing you'll feel something
like a sliver in your heart.

Though you're thrilled beyond description
that your baby's now a bride,
you will have a strange sensation
like an itch deep down inside.

It's a bittersweetish splinter
that you cannot tweezer out
cause it's wedged and twisted sideways.
It's what good grief's all about.

It's a shard that's caused by memories
of those precious years you had
planting seeds of faith and wisdom
as her mentor, as her dad.

It's a sliver that you'll live with.
You'll thank God that it is there
for it's just one more reminder
what you've shared is really rare.

Within four years of handing the coach my little poem, it was my turn to walk my middle daughter down the aisle. I discovered that what I had imagined was going through the coach's mind was spot-on. That was back in 2011, but I still remember the lump in my throat and the tear in my eye.

And this weekend I will once again have an opportunity to put into practice the advice I've given countless other fathers-of-the-bride. This time it's my baby girl who will be pledging a lifetime of love to the man of her dreams. In anticipation of the center aisle stroll Lauren and I will be taking, I've reread the words I composed for Mike Holmgren seventeen years ago. And even though I'm the one who wrote them, they speak to me of the sacredness of what's ahead.

Poetry is like that. There is something about rhyming words and phrases that capture what prose often can't. The emotions that dance in the heart of a bride (and her father) on her wedding day are more easily described in word pictures. In the forty-five years I've been a pastor, I have used poetry to create such portraits of life's sacred moments. The birth of a baby. The death of a parent. The completion of a degree. A couple's engagement. Unexpected unemployment. A job promotion. A doctor's dreaded diagnosis. Or even a coach's Super Bowl victory (or defeat).

But for this weekend, I'm taking my own medicine and practicing what I've preached.

Never Underestimate the Power of the Past

Recently I came across a letter a pastoral mentor mailed me thirty-one years ago. It was from Bud Palmberg, the longtime beloved pastor of the Covenant church on Mercer Island. Even though I was serving a church in California at the time, I'd known Bud from years before when I pastored a church in Seattle as a young unmarried cleric. Every Monday on the golf course, he provided me encouragement and insight pertaining to a career I was just beginning.

In 1993, after giving leadership to the Mercer Island congregation for twenty-six years, Bud and his wife Donna accepted a call to the International Church in Luzern Switzerland. His letter to me described what his new parish was like. I was fascinated by what he detailed. The Palmbergs would spent the next seven years of their lives at that English-speaking church in Central Switzerland.

When I received Bud's letter in 1993, I had no way of knowing that a dozen years later I would become the lead pastor at the Mercer Island Covenant Church where he'd served for a quarter century. Neither could I have known that I would be called to that same English-speaking church in Switzerland to serve as interim pastor. That three-month experience in Luzern was one of the highlights in my forty-five-year career.

Looking back I can now see how circumstances of my past set in motion a series of events that God would use to guide my steps. A friendship with Bud Palmberg that began forty-five years ago would result in unanticipated blessings. But that's not all.

Recently I admitted to a friend that my ten years as chaplain at a local retirement community were the most fulfilling season of my ministry. And looking back I can see why. In that role I was allowed to use my unique gifts and creative abilities to live out my call. Experiences from my past had prepared me for what my job description demanded of me.

As an elementary school kid my pastor-father allowed me to tag along with him as he did visits to elderly members who were housebound. He asked me to pass out hymnbooks at the nursing home each month as he led a Sunday afternoon worship service. In college I did a research project that explored options to help vision impaired senior adults read the Bible.

When my dad went on hospice fifteen years ago, I observed intently what all was involved in caring for the dying. I had no idea that five years later I would be a chaplain helping residents on our campus pack their bags for heaven on a regular basis. The same was true with regard to my mom. As my brother and I slowly walked with her through the dark tunnel of dementia, I realized I was learning firsthand what I would need to know as a chaplain a few years later when I spent much time in our memory care wing.

But I am not the only one who can attest to the benefits of experiences and contacts earlier in our lives. If we take the time to reflect on our past, most everyone would acknowledge the same payoff. The investments of years gone by have resulted in compounded interest and dividends beyond what we could have dreamed. Opportunities and open doors we credit with the most meaningful moments in our lives did not exist in a vacuum. They likely were tied to something we did or someone we met sometime back.

And we'd best not forget that certain Someone who choreographs life's circumstances in such a way that the connections of our past pave the way for our future. That's why I am attracted to the words I read in the eighth chapter of St. Paul's Letter to the Romans. And we know that in all things God works for the good of those who love him, who have been called according to his purpose.

Yes, our past experiences really do contribute to our current blessings.

Returning an Overdue Book

During Christmas break 2005, I visited my favorite thrift store near my in-laws in Southern California. What I discovered was a treasure that meant as much as any gift I'd received beneath the tree.

There on a dusty bookshelf was a slender antique volume entitled "Nearer My God to Thee." That old hymn reminded me of the Titanic's tragic voyage. As you may have read, while the famous ship was sinking, the band remained on deck playing that poignant melody.

I opened the fly leaf of the book and noticed a handwritten inscription. The beautiful script acknowledged the 8th birthday of Francis Griset and the date of his birth. July 14, 1911. It was signed by one of Francis' grandmothers. Because I was already thinking of the Titanic, it struck me that this young boy was born just nine months before the infamous vessel struck an iceberg on April 14, 1912. As I held the book and focused on the personal inscription, I felt as if I had found buried treasure. And to top it off, my find was only 99 cents.

For the past nineteen years that little treasure has been a valued part of my collection of Titanic memorabilia that includes a plastic model of the ship and several books that document the disaster. I have displayed the book as an illustration whenever I have preached one of my favorite sermons: "Spiritual Lessons from a Sinking Ship." In a newspaper column I wrote three months ago referring to the Titanic, I referenced my antique book including a photo.

Upon my return to the States from three months in Switzerland, I was retrieving a boatload of voicemails on my landline. One message stopped me in my tracks. It was from a man by the name of Jim Griset. His brief message indicated that someone had sent him one of my newspaper columns. He went on to say that it was an article about a book I'd found in a thrift store inscribed to a Francis Griset. In his recorded message he informed me that Francis was his father. I was stunned.

Returning his call, I thanked Jim for reaching out to me. He told me about his dad who had died in 2005. Upon asking more about his father, I discovered that Francis was only nine months old when his twenty-four year old mother died (ironically on the same day the Titanic went down).

Jim told me it was Francis' maternal grandmother who inscribed the book to him on his eighth birthday. Quite conceivably she gave the boy the book because of what it represented. It's quite possible the hymn and the book were meaningful to her because of its connection to the Titanic story. After all, she lost her daughter (Francis' mother) to death on the same day 1,500 lives were lost in the North Atlantic.

In our conversation I was fascinated to learn that Jim's father and my wife's parents (although they never met) lived in the same community and both attended Presbyterians churches. I told Jim that my in-laws were career missionaries with Wycliffe Bible Translators started by William Cameron Townsend. He told me that his dad was actually related to the Townsend family. Another small world connection!

Jim related to me that as his dad grew older, he would often play hymns for his father on the piano. Ironically it was the very piano given to Francis' mother before he was born by the same grandmother who gave him the book. Jim told me his dad loved it when he played

"Nearer My God to Thee." What he'd received as a child had taken root deep in his young heart. And for good reason.

As Jim continued to share information about his dad, something else dawned on me. Francis received the book from his grandmother in the summer of 1919 during the Spanish Flu pandemic when people were dying throughout the nation. That beloved hymn must have offered comfort to young Francis just as they had to the grieving woman who had given the book to him.

When Jim and I finished our conversation, it was clear what I had to do. With joy I mailed the book to its rightful owner.

A Blueprint for Success

Fifteen years ago last month our youngest daughter graduated from Mercer Island High School. Because I was a pastor in the community at the time, I was included in the baccalaureate program. The keynote speaker was Ed Pepple, the legendary basketball coach at the high school. Ed had just retired after 42 years at MIHS in which he led the Islanders to four state championships.

Although I did not know "Coach" personally, I was aware that his son Kyle taught school in my hometown of Wenatchee. As the father of one of the graduates, I listened intently to what Ed shared from my daughter's perspective. The winningest high school basketball coach in Washington State history offered lessons he'd learned in his stellar career.

Having just lost my dad a few months before, I was alert to the coach's fatherlike advice. He called his life lessons *"A Blueprint for Success."* Even though I heard him give his talk fifteen years ago, I've kept the notes to presentation on my laptop ever since.

Ed's *"Blueprint for Success"* included the following twenty bullet points:

1. *Be a giver, not a taker.*
2. *Have enthusiasm for everything you do.*
3. *All setbacks are temporary because obstacles are only steppingstones to success.*
4. *Give extra effort and always do more than is necessary.*

5. Accept responsibility for all of your actions because excuses are for losers.
6. Put first things first by prioritizing.
7. Think positively about everything.
8. Practice random acts of kindness.
9. Leaders and champions are made and not born.
10. If you always tell the truth, there is less to remember.
11. It is amazing what can be accomplished when no one cares who gets the credit.
12. Make dust or eat dust. You are not in competition with others.
13. Value your friends and never let them down.
14. Know how to accept a compliment because if you reject them you'll cease to get them and compliments are GOOD things.
15. Be willing to compromise.
16. Better to shoot high and miss than to shoot low and hit your mark.
17. It takes as much energy to wish as it does to plan.
18. Choose your friends wisely because they are like the buttons on an elevator. They will either take you up or take you down.
19. Time is the greatest gift of all so don't waste it. The bad news is that time flies. The good news is that you are the pilot.
20. No rain means no rainbows.

After his retirement from coaching, Ed Pepple became a friend of mine. We had a mutual friend in Gary Snyder (whose son Quin had played for Ed back in the eighties). Gary included me in his visits with "Coach." We enjoyed breakfast periodically at The Pancake Corral where there was an item on the menu named for him.

Early on in our friendship, Ed told me that his wife Shirley was a faithful reader of my newspaper columns. I was humbled. From that point on I felt the permission to relate to the legend as a peer. He never tired of boasting about his grandson Matt Logie who had followed in his footsteps as a standout basketball coach.

When Ed was diagnosed with cancer our visits included a spiritual component. Although quiet about his faith, he allowed me to pray with him. When he passed away in 2020 at the age of 88, Ed's wife

Shirley welcomed me into the family circle as their personal chaplain. COVID restrictions prevented what would have been standing-room only celebration of life of a man who left his mark on countless lives and on our community.

Recently I learned that there is talk about the possibility of naming the Mercer Island High School basketball court after Ed. I don't know what all would be involved in bringing about such a tribute, but I hope it comes to pass. I also hope it happens while Ed's wife is still alive to witness what would be a most worthy acknowledgement of one of Washington State's greatest sports personalities. In the meantime, I'm

Lessons from "The Boys in the Boat"

My wife and I crossed the finish line of 2023 by going to see "The Boys in the Boat." Given the fact that the theater wasn't far from the University of Washington campus and on the same weekend as the UW football team won the right to compete in the national championship, the atmosphere was electric.

Seeing the movie on the big screen reminded me of a lazy Saturday morning ten years ago when I had coffee with Daniel Brown (the author of the book on which the movie is based). My motivation in getting together with him was to have him sign a rowing poster for my brother. Marc had been a coxswain for the Seattle Pacific University crew team. During our visit, Daniel described the lengthy and complicated process it would take should his story ever make it to the big screen.

My brother's experience at our alma mater was my first introduction to the sport of rowing. I was amazed at the arduous training and strict discipline required to compete at the collegiate level. And I was so proud of my kid brother who ran the five miles and worked out each day at 5am with his oarsmen. Although coxswains don't need to be as physically fit as the rowers, Marc joined his team in their daily regimen in order to earn their respect. As a result of his willingness to endure the torturous training with them, they willingly took direction from his 5'6" 130 pound frame during competitions.

My next exposure to rowing came four decades later. I discovered that Carl Lovsted, one of the members of Mercer Island Covenant Church where I was pastor, had won a bronze medal in the 1952 Summer Olympics with the University of Washington four-man crew team. After some coaxing, Carl finally showed me his medal. I was impressed by his humble "aw-shucks" attitude toward such an amazing achievement.

And then in 2013 my wife and I read Daniel Brown's just-released book about the UW rowing team winning a gold medal in the 1936 Summer Olympics in Berlin. After hearing the author speak, I asked for the privilege of meeting with him over coffee. Not only did Daniel arrange his schedule to meet with me, he directed me to the daughter of Joe Rantz about whom "The Boys in the Boat" is primarily concerned. Judy Rantz Willman willingly accepted my invitation to talk about her celebrated father at the retirement center where I was the chaplain.

A few years later when my friend Carl died, his family asked me to officiate the memorial service at the Conibear Rowing House at the University of Washington campus. I could not have been more honored. Directly above me was the Husky Clipper (in which the 1936 team had won Olympic gold) suspended from the ceiling.

My various exposures to rowing over the past five decades proceeded to play out on the walls of my memories as I watched George Clooney's brilliant motion picture on the big screen. As I observed the themes in the film of overcoming adversity, self-denial and teamwork I couldn't help but recognize similar themes I've read about and preached from in the New Testament.

In the Gospel accounts of Jesus and his disciples, we find another group of "boys in a boat." Like the Husky crew of 1936, those first century fishermen struggled with individualism, pride and failure. Like the ragtag wannabees that UW coach Al Ulbrickson transformed into a winning team, the boys in the boat in which Jesus invested were an unreliable group of hotheads. They sought personal glory. And similar to Bobby Mock, the UW coxswain, the rabbi from Nazareth called out self-destructive tendencies and coached them to deny self that they might discover unity. Refusing to simply let them look out for themselves, Jesus repeatedly provided a rhythm of oneness He himself modeled.

In the book and in the movie, the Husky crew team experienced a unity that propelled them to victory much to Hitler's chagrin. In the New Testament version of "the boys in the boat," Jesus' crew overcame their ego-driven personalities in a show of humility and service. Their devotion and discipline culminated in a movement that would shape the values of justice and morality that continue to be embraced two millennia later. It's called Christianity.

The Impressions We Leave Behind

They are called ghost signs. Before billboards became the prominent form of outdoor advertising, hand-painted signs on the sides of buildings were the norm. Some have disappeared with the demolition of the bricks on which they were originally painted. Others have become unreadable with the passage of time. Still others remain quite visible. The ghost sign on the side of the Liberty Theater is one that is quite prominent. It's a time capsule of sorts. It calls to mind a much simpler season of life.

There are other ghost signs in Wenatchee. I recall seeing ones that advertise Swift Premium meats, Wiester Department Store, Morris Hardware and Huggins Shoes. On my drive from Mercer Island to Wenatchee, I see other ghost signs in Cle Elum. It would make for a fun "treasure hunt" on a rainy day. I find the search for such signs fascinating. I also find it symbolic.

Ghost signs speak to me of lasting impressions. In addition to offering a snapshot of the past, they picture what remains long after something has become a victim of time. In a very real sense, memories we have of people (and the memories they have of us) are a kind of ghost sign.

You've probably heard the expression, "What matters most is not what we did or what we said but how we made someone feel." In other words, the lasting impression we leave behind is what others hold on to the most.

A couple weeks ago a friend and mentor passed away at the age of eighty. I first met Ed Smyth in the fall of 1975 when he joined the faculty in the school of religion at Seattle Pacific University. As a recent graduate wrestling with a call to the ministry, I reached out to Ed for help in clarifying next steps. The fact that he was eight years older than I provided him a perspective that proved helpful. Over lunches at a favorite Chinese restaurant, Ed challenged me to do the hard work of self-inventory.

Since our first meeting nearly fifty years ago, Ed continued to invest in my life. I still have handwritten letters in his slanted lefthanded scrawl that he mailed me when I was in seminary. When I served my first church following seminary, I asked Ed to be a guest preacher and facilitate a workshop of discipleship. He willingly complied. As he spent time with our congregation and watched me in action, he affirmed my call.

Years and miles would eventually separate our lives, but periodic opportunities to connect resulted in feelings of love, acceptance and affirmation. Ed remained a touchstone of my call to ministry.

The week prior to his death, Ed's wife texted me acknowledging the end was near. She invited me to share special memories that she could relay to him while he remained conscious. Ellen indicated that countless individuals, who knew death was near, had called, emailed and traveled cross-country to honor a much-loved man. She was blown away by Ed's influence on the lives of so many.

Following his passing, I was amazed at the tributes that were posted on Ed's Facebook page. Friends, colleagues and former students eulogized this most amazing man with unsolicited references to the impact he'd had on their lives. Their posts validated the fact that Ed had made them feel special. It was obvious that his impact was a "ghost sign" that would not quickly fade.

Looking back, I can't honestly recall specific things that Ed Smyth said. I've forgotten things that he did or taught. But I will never forget how he made me feel. And I'm grateful those feelings are positive ones.

Looking ahead, I want my life to engender a similar response. It won't bother me if former members of my congregations can't recall sermons

I've preached. It won't matter to me if no one can recite poems I've published. I won't even be frustrated that longtime friends still can't pronounce my last name. What will matter the most is that those who recall my life will do so with a sense of gratitude. Like ghost signs on Wenatchee buildings, I want to leave a lasting impression.

Faces in the Forest

When my wife and I were vacationing at our family cottage on Lake Chelan a few years ago, we took an early morning walk among a grove of trees. I looked up and saw what appeared to be two eyes looking at me. What appeared to be a camouflaged countenance were actually knots in the trunk of a maple tree. They resembled the face of a deer. Amazed by what I saw, I captured the Bambi-like pose on my iPhone. The unexpected image inspired a column for my weekly newspaper assignment. Since that time, I have seen a plethora of faces on rocks, in bushes and on tree trunks.

I started collecting photos of faces in the forest on my iPhone. The more I added to my collection, the more I realized I needed to do something with them. And then the idea hit me. A year or so ago I published an interactive walking journal with photos of poems I had written on paper bags and tacked to a tree in a nearby park. Why not do another walking journal with photos of the natural faces I've photographed? And so I have done just that.

Faces in the Forest is a compilation of the photos taken with my iPhone along with Biblical quotes about nature, hymn lyrics celebrating creation and original poetry about the stewardship of our environment. There are also ample blank pages for the purpose of reflecting on the beauty of the outdoors and writing personal observations.

Looking back, I believe that my fascination with finding faces in the forest is due in part to the fact that my father was a minister. Being raised in a pastor's home, I grew up being exposed to Scripture. I knew that *"the eyes of the Lord run to and fro throughout the whole earth…"* Daily family devotions reminded me of that.

Memorizing passages from the Bible was an expectation as well as a personal challenge. Those verses that personally "spoke" to me were easier to commit to memory. As someone who enjoyed poetry from a young age, I especially related to portions of God's Word that utilized similes and metaphors. As I read Scripture, I realized the importance of visualizing truth in creative ways.

In the Old Testament there is the poetic use of language describing nature anthropomorphically. As a young person I resonated with the prophet Isaiah's description of redemption's drama. The playwright portrays God's people walking onto the stage of creation against the backdrop of props the Master Set Designer had created. All living things are viewed as cast members along with us as the lead actors who are created in the image of their Creator.

You will go out in joy and be led forth in peace;
the mountains and hills will burst into song before you,
and all the trees of the field will clap their hands. (Isaiah 55:12)

Long before Rogers and Hammerstein suggested that the hills are alive with the sound of music, Isaiah was celebrating that reality. And trees applauding their praise of the Creator? What a profound (yet simple) picture of how our lives are interrelated to all living things.

My illustrated walking journal is intended to call attention to "our friends" with whom we share life. I invite the reader to be alert to see "faces" on tree trunks or on rocks or in bushes that remind us of the fact that all nature is alive with the essence of God's presence. The world around us is animated with the pulsating beauty of life. Plants, trees, brooks and rivers along with birds, rabbits and squirrels that meet us in the forest are companions with us on a planet for which we have been called to care.

As you go for walks and hikes with Mother Nature, be aware of your Heavenly Father's fingerprints. Look for the unexpected nuances that point to our connection with all living things. In all honesty, you don't need my walking journal to capture what you find. All you need is a willingness to focus on what's in front of you.

A Tribute to a Timeless Carroll

I first learned that Pete Carroll was being replaced as the Seahawks head coach from my oldest daughter. Kristin posted team owner Jody Allen's memo on our family text thread. Getting that kind of news from our daughter was not a surprise. In addition to being our clan's NFL insider, Kristin is the consummate 12. Daughter #1 is always in-the-know when it comes to everything that relates to the Seahawks. Even though she lives and works at a large church in Southern California, Kristin remains devoted to her hometown team. Understandably, my daughter was devastated by the news of Pete's departure. And Kristin's sadness was shared by our entire family.

For fourteen years Coach Carroll's upbeat positive personality had provided us an example of how to view a glass half-full. His youthful presence and upbeat leadership was optimism personified. I couldn't imagine not seeing Pete on the sidelines on Sundays in the fall. I felt the need to process my grief. And as I often do (when something of significance occurs), I grabbed my laptop and proceeded to express my feelings with words.

Since the news about Pete broke as we were packing up our holiday decorations, songs of the season were still playing in my mind. I couldn't help but thinking of Pete Carroll as just another one of the carols that I love this time of year. As I thought about "this friend I'd never met," the following phrases from popular Christmas carols came to mind and I wrote…

On many a bleak midwinter
Pete brought joy to our world.
But on this silent night,
not even Good King Wenceslas
has a smile on his face.
O come all ye faithful 12s.
Acknowledge your sorrow.
Voice your gratitude.
A much-loved Carroll has been deleted from our playlist.
And the soundtrack that has been such an indispensable part
of our season of celebration is missing.
Nonetheless, I'm grateful for this timeless Carroll
who will remain in our hearts even as we continue to sing his praises!

Much like the carols we sing in church or hear on the radio, Pete Carroll was an earworm. The sound of his voice triggered joy. He endeared himself to our community. His presence prompted us to want to "sing along" and embrace his enthusiasm for life. Even though this beloved coach is six months older than I am, his energy leaves me envious (And I'm a fairly energetic seventy-one-year-old).

Seeing how Coach Pete has been praised by players and fans alike, got me to thinking about what will be said about me when I leave "the locker room of life." What will I be known for? What will be remembered? Will my name be an earworm that brings joy to the world I leave behind?

Do you ever think about such things? Do you wonder what the person who will one day give your eulogy will say? With that in mind, I'm reminded of a book on my bedstead written by New York Times columnist David Brooks. In "The Road to Character," the author makes a case for the importance of *eulogy virtues* over *resume virtues*. As you might expect, the former is far more important than the latter.

Pete Carroll's involvement in the community, as well as on the practice field, demonstrated his determined desire to put others first. His sensitivity to those with whom he came in contact was reflected in his willingness to take the be "present" with them. Both in college football and in the pros, Pete was building his eulogy virtues by not being deterred by delayed gratification or unexpected setbacks.

As I contemplate Pete Carroll's success, I'm reminded what Jesus said about loving your neighbor as you love yourself. As I reflect on the coach's contagious personality, I realize this Carroll really is like a Christmas carol. It starts to play several weeks before the holiday season. It's largely upbeat. It's memorable. It triggers happy thoughts. And it calls to mind memorable messages.

Observing Pete's influence as a coach, I'm reminded of the following axiom. *"People will not remember what you did as much as they will remember how you made them feel."*

More Than a Christmas Card

Did you know that timeless holiday film *It's a Wonderful Life* began as a Christmas card? It's true. Two years after Philip Van Doren Stern sent his novella as a greeting card to his family and friends in 1943, it fell into the hands of Hollywood director Frank Capra. As a result, the world was introduced to George Bailey of Bedford Falls.

Some of the carols we enjoy listening to and singing this time of the year began as Christmas cards as well. These carols include *Some Children See Him*, *Caroling, Caroling*, and *The Star Carol*. These much-loved contemporary Christmas carols were written by Alfred Burt.

Alfred Burt was the son of a Michigan minister who wrote original Christmas carols each year. Beginning in 1922, Reverend Bates Burt would send the lyrics and music to his family and congregation as his personal Christmas card. When Alfred Burt graduated with a degree in music from the University of Michigan in 1942, his pastor-father asked his son to write the music for the carols while the elder Burt continued to compose the lyrics. Alfred was thrilled to collaborate with his dad.

That collaboration only lasted six years, however, when Reverend Burt suddenly died of a heart attack in 1948. The younger Burt, now married, decided with his wife to continue the family tradition. Alfred asked his father's church organist if she would be willing to write the lyrics for each year's carol. Wihla Hutson agreed.

Wihla and Alfred's first joint venture was *Sleep Baby Mine*. When Alfred's wife Anne discovered she was expecting their first child, Anne requested Whila to write the 1949 Christmas lyric as a lullaby. It would celebrate the Savior's birth as well as be used to announce the birth of the Burt addition in March of 1950.

Shortly after daughter Diane was born, the family of three moved from Michigan to Southern California. Alfred was in demand as a studio musician. His abilities as a composer were only overshadowed by his skill as a jazz trumpet player. As part of Alvino Rey's Orchestra, Alfred traveled the country performing as well as arranging for recordings and television programs.

His career was on a fast track. Still, the holiday music of Alfred Burt and Wihla Hutson was not gaining much recognition. It was mostly known by those on the family Christmas card list. A group of less than five hundred individuals.

And then the unexpected. Alfred Burt celebrated Christmas of 1953 with his family knowing it would be his last. This gifted musician (who served as the assistant choir director at his church) had been diagnosed with advanced lung cancer a few months earlier. He was making peace with the fact that he would likely die at the age of thirty-three, just like the Jewish carpenter's son whose birth we commemorate at Christmas.

Sitting in a wheelchair, a weak Alfred Burt sat in a Southern California church conducting Hollywood's most gifted musicians for a recording session. They were capturing his collection of original Christmas carols on reel-to-reel tape. Carols that would not become part of our holiday repertoire for years to come.

That recording session resulted in a long-play vinyl album titled *The Christmas Mood* produced by Columbia Records and was released after his death in 1954. It included *The Star Carol*, the last carol on which he and Wihla Hutson would collaborate. Alfred actually finished the music less than twenty-four hours before he died.

Because Alfred Burt approached the Christmas of 1953 overshadowed by a doctor's grim diagnosis, his musical offering provided a sense of healing in the midst of personal heartache. His creativity served his hope. His faith sustained his declining health. Just as it had when he and his wife lost their second child in a miscarriage.

As one raised in the church, Alfred was aware that the message of the season is tinged with both joy and sorrow. He knew the baby's cry from a cradle and the Savior's sigh from a cross are part of the same story. The child in the manger is one who was born to die for our flawed humanity and our broken world. Such a truth is worth pondering this season while listening to some of Alfred Burt's music.

Let's Talk About Angels

"Every time a bell rings an angel gets his wings." Most everyone I know recognizes that iconic line from Frank Capra's timeless Christmas film *"It's a Wonderful Life."* But not all. The other night after a dinner of Buffalo wings (a perfect pre-movie menu, right?), I had the privilege of introducing my millennial daughter's fiancé to this holiday classic for the first time.

It was a hoot to see Scotty's reaction to Clarence Odbody AS2. He's the second-class wingless angel who gives a despondent do-gooder by the name of George Bailey a glimpse as to what the world would have been like had he never been born. At that turning point in the movie, the father of four realizes what a wonderful life he has in spite of his tribulations. By helping George Bailey focus on his blessings, Clarence is awarded his wings at last.

I love that feel-good film. The final scene finds me wiping tears from my eyes every time. But as a man-of-the-cloth I find the theological treatment of angels a bit frayed. The Scriptures do not suggest that angels can successfully earn their wings any more than humans can successfully earn their salvation. And furthermore, although cherubim and seraphim are pictured in the prophet Isaiah's vision as having three pairs of wings (Isaiah chapter 6), there is no basis for believing that all angelic beings possess wings.

My wife's favorite holiday movie also features Cary Grant portraying an angel at Christmastime. In *"The Bishop's Wife,"* Dudley is dispatched to the home of a New York City cleric. The angelic visitor becomes romantically infatuated with the bishop's spouse while trying to accomplish his mission. Again, nowhere in the Bible is such a scenario of angelic romance suggested. Angels have a singular purpose.

The Greek word *angelos* that is translated *angel* in the New Testament simply means messenger. Angels are supernatural beings who communicate a divine message from God. And in the Christmas story angels play a major role. Just think of it. An angel informs Mary that she will become pregnant. An angel visits Mary's fiancé in a dream and informs Joseph he should not break off his engagement even though his unmarried future wife is expecting a baby that is not his. Also, an angel encounters Zechariah, the husband of Mary's cousin, and tells him that his infertile older wife will finally be able to conceive.

But perhaps the most familiar account of angels in the Christmas story relates to the night that Jesus is born. There are angels that appear in the sky that proceed to scare the living daylights out of a group of shepherds on a hillside outside of Bethlehem. And even though their message was *"Fear not!"* I'm guessing they were still shaking in their sandals.

No wonder the music of the Christmas season includes a disproportional number of carols that refer to angels. For example, there's *"Hark the Herald Angels," "Angels We Have Heard on High," "Angels from the Realms of Glory," "O Come All Ye Faithful"* and *"The First Noel."*

There's really no way to contemplate this sacred season without giving angels their appropriate due. They serve as tangible pointers to the message of love. Whether it's an old black-and-white holiday movie or readings as the candles of the Advent wreath are lit in church, angels call attention to what we dare not forget.

There's another Christmas angel in my frame of reference. It's a piece of painted Mexican pottery. I purchased it a couple days after Christmas when I got engaged forty-two years ago. I gave that little angel as an expression of thanks to my future in-laws for giving me their blessing to marry their eldest daughter. Because Wendy had grown up in Mexico City with her missionary family, it seemed an appropriate object. And that angel still sits on a bookshelf in her parents' living room all these year later.

That angel reminds me of my love for my wife and her love for me. It reminds me of my love for my in-laws who soon will celebrate seventy-three years of marriage. But most of all that little Mexican angel recalls God's love for a world He entered as a baby more than two millennia ago. I guess you could say, every time I see that angel, a bell goes off in my head reminding me how much I am loved.

Redemption: A Case Study

Recently I stopped at our local thrift store. I was in search of a couple unique items to add to our "Santa Closet." That's what we call our guest bathroom when it is decorated with my collection of Santas. My trip was a success. In addition to a couple small miniature Santa figures, I found a reproduction of the original first edition copy of Clement C. Moore's "The Night Before Christmas." It was only 99 cents.

But before I left the store, my eyes locked on something I wasn't expecting. What I saw caught me by surprise. To be honest, it was quite humbling. There on a shelf with other Christmas decorator items was a beautifully framed poem I had written.

The poem, illustrated by a calligrapher friend, was inspired by my favorite holiday movie "It's a Wonderful Life." I loved the way it turned out. I loved it so much I had framed copies made that I sold (along with books I have written about the movie) when I've appeared at the annual "It's a Wonderful Life Festival" in Seneca Falls, New York. That what locals call "the real Bedford Falls."

But what was my framed poem doing in our local thrift store? Perhaps I had given it as a hostess gift when my wife and I were entertained at some home during the holidays. And because they didn't like it as much as I did, they dropped it off with other unwanted items. Maybe I had given it to as a birthday present to a resident at the retirement community where I worked as chaplain. When that person passed away, it's possible their family donated items to the local thrift store when emptying out the apartment.

Humbled by the reality that my gift had likely been discarded, I began to reflect on the how humility is baked into the message of the Christmas story. The teenage mother of Jesus was humbled when told she'd been chosen to give birth to the Son of God. Facing the scorn of townsfolk for being in the family way without the benefit of marriage was far more humbling then than it is today.

Likewise, Joseph was no doubt humiliated when he discovered his fiancé was pregnant. After all, he knew it couldn't be his child. Swallowing his pride, he chose to stand with Mary although unable to explain her situation to those in his sphere of influence.

The Apostle Paul also connects the concept of humility to the incarnation story. He calls Christ followers to follow His example by being willing to give up their rights and feelings of privilege. He claims that this is what Jesus did by being born a human baby.

In his letter to the first century church in Philippi, Paul writes, *"In your relationships with one another, have the same mindset as Christ Jesus: Who, being in very nature[a] God, did not consider equality with God something to be used to his own advantage; rather, he made himself nothing by taking the very nature[b] of a servant, being made in human likeness. And being found in appearance as a man, he humbled himself by becoming obedient to death—even death on a cross!"* (Philippians 2:5-8)

Although initially humbled by finding my framed art in the thrift store, I now was humbled to realize I might be blaming the wrong people. Reflecting on the situation, it occurred to me that I might have inadvertently included that prized item in one of several bags to be donated after cleaning out my garage. Perhaps I was the one responsible. Alexa, how do you spell *eggonmyface*?

Well, I wasn't going to leave my framed IAWL poem at the store. But it was no longer mine to simply take home. To reclaim it, I had to purchase it. I added that which had once been mine to my basket of Santa Closet décor and made my way to the cashier. I had redeemed what I had lost.

Driving home with my reclaimed possession, the thought occurred to me "Redemption is also at the center of the Christmas story, too!" The reason God came to us as one of us was the buy back a treasured possession He couldn't imagine spending eternity without.

The Unsent Christmas Card

This is the week I finalize our family Christmas card and start stamping and addressing envelopes. It's a labor-intensive task, but it's an annual holiday tradition I really enjoy. Designing a custom card and writing an original Christmas poem provides a creative soul like me with a platform for sharing my heart with friends and family. The cost of sending out close to a hundred cards adds up. Especially when you consider the price of materials, photos and postage. But it's worth it to me. It's a gift I give myself.

I come from a long line of Christmas card senders. My mom was a conscientious correspondent. So was her mother. Communicating the "good news of great joy" that this season represents (in terms of our faith and our family) is at the heart of the holiday. Christmas couldn't be Christmas without sending Christmas cards.

Recently, while sorting through a box of family memorabilia, I came across an addressed envelope that had never been mailed. I recognized the name. When I tore open the envelope, I discovered it was a Christmas card my grandmother had intended to send to her brother sixty years ago. Sadly, he never received it. Not long after addressing the unsent card, my grandmother began to struggle with dementia. As a result, her tradition of sending Christmas cards came to an end

Because my great-uncle and his wife lived within the state, I'm fairly certain my grandmother had opportunity to convey her affection to her brother in subsequent to that Christmas season. But finding that unmailed card got me to thinking of the importance of telling people that we care about how we feel about them while we can.

Life has a way of complicating our best intentions for communicating our love. Friends and family move away. Friends and family die unexpectedly. Our ability to verbalize our feelings (as in the case of my Nana's memory-loss) may evaporate. And those we could have communicated with may very well lose their ability to remember who we are once we finally get around to letting them know.

This month as extended family members gather for gift-exchanges and holiday meals, there will be empty chairs in living rooms and empty places at dinner tables. Those vacancies will call to mind those who have left us through the doorway of death since last we gathered. And in many cases, there will be silent sighs of regret for not having had one last opportunity to say "I love you!"

Like an unsent Christmas card or unmailed birthday card, unspoken expressions of affection are missed chances to remind someone special that we really think they are. When we realize we blew it, we hope we'll have another chance. And I guess this column is a call to action. It's my hope that you take advantage of the chance you have this Christmas to remind someone what they mean to you.

The message of Christmas for those who follow the Christian faith is essentially this: The Creator of the universe didn't assume those created in His image understood they were loved. Instead, he became a human Christmas card conveying His love. This priority mail envelope was personally delivered complete with a tracking number and fully insured. And while this one-of-a-kind Christmas card was delivered, there is no guarantee that it has been opened by those to whom it was addressed. That remains a personal decision.

What if Jesus Had Never Been Born?

When Philip Van Doren Stern's 4,000-word short story "The Greatest Gift" failed to impress a prospective publisher, the writer and Civil War historian decided to print it himself. He sent it out as his Christmas card to family and friends in December 1943. The story had to do with a despondent man contemplating suicide who is given the opportunity to see what the world would have been like had he never been born.

One of those who happened upon this unique Christmas greeting was Hollywood director Frank Capra who bought the movie rights to the story for $10,000. Capra adapted *The Greatest Gift* into a screenplay and gave Stern's story a new title. *It's a Wonderful Life* was released as a motion picture in December, 1946.

What originated as a Christmas card became a movie released at Christmastime. And each Christmastime, *It's a Wonderful Life* is shown multiple times. If it wasn't for Christmas, we would never know the story of George Bailey. But more significantly, without Christmas our world would be drastically different.

British writer C. S. Lewis imagined such a dark, Christ-less planet in his brilliant children's story *The Lion, the Witch and the Wardrobe*. The world he conceived he called Narnia. Paralyzed under the frozen spell of the White Witch, it is a world in which it is "always winter but never Christmas."

A world in which it is always winter but never Christmas would be a world in which the mail carrier stuffs your box with bills, bank statements, and third-class junk. No Christmas would mean no Christmas cards or caroling or gift giving. The world would be devoid of twinkling lights and festive decorations. By definition, a world without Christmas would be a world without Jesus.

The shock George Bailey felt as he wandered into the dark and depraved city limits of Pottersville is nothing when compared with what we would feel if our sin-infested planet had been denied the "Light of the World." What worked as a brilliant literary motif in Stern's story works as a startling exercise for those tempted to approach their faith casually. We would do well to ponder what our world would be like had Jesus Christ never been born.

If Jesus had never been born, not only would there be no Christmas, there would be no Valentine's Day, St. Patrick's Day, Mardi Gras, Easter, Halloween, or Thanksgiving. Each one of those popular American holidays is based on (or somehow tied to) Christianity. But a world without Jesus would have even greater implications.

Can you imagine a world without the artistic masterpieces of the Renaissance largely influenced by the Christian message? Can you imagine a world without a boat named the Mayflower transporting victims of religious persecution to the New World determined to populate a land where faith could be freely practiced? Can you imagine a world without William Wilberforce and his Christian witness against slavery in Britain's Parliament?

Can you imagine a world without George Frederic Handel's immortal oratorio *Messiah*? Can you imagine science textbooks that do not include the findings of Copernicus, Kepler, Galileo, Descartes, Pascal, Newton, Faraday, and Mendel all of whom embraced the Christ of history and were shaped by his teachings?

Can you imagine a world without universities like Oxford, Cambridge, Harvard, Yale, Princeton, and many others that were founded by Christians to train Christians? Can you imagine a world without Clara Barton and the lifesaving efforts that came from her Red Cross? Can you imagine a world without General William Booth and his army of soldiers fighting on the frontlines of homelessness, hunger, and poverty? Can you imagine a world without Bill Wilson's Twelve Steps or his Big Blue Book or the countless lives who have regained sobriety through the organization called Alcoholics Anonymous?

And furthermore, if Jesus had never been born, we would not have the assurance of forgiveness and confidence of the Creator's acceptance and the wonderful life we were created to experience.

The Difference a Day Makes

It didn't dawn on me until just recently that Leap Year always coincides with the year we elect a President. It's also the same year the Summer Olympics are held. Every fourth year we gain an extra day. And with all that takes place every fourth year, it's probably a good thing we are given more time to process what's going on around us.

As we've been told, leap year occurs because Earth's orbit around the sun and its rotation on its axis are not perfectly in line. It takes our planet 365.24 days to orbit the sun, but our Gregorian calendar consists of 365 days. So, in order to synchronize the calendar with the solar year, an extra day is added every four years.

So how do you spend that additional day? Do you treat it as a personal holiday and take it off from work? Or perhaps you have family traditions that have evolved over the years that you observe on the 29th day of February. Have you ever thought of latching on to Leap Year as a means of creating a custom that is unique to the sphere of influence who orbit your life?

Given the divisive and contentious nature of the Presidential campaign, this bonus day might well be used as an opportunity to pray for unity in our nation as the election season plays out. Even though the first Thursday in May is recognized each year as the National Day of Prayer, perhaps we could use a second day of prayer for our country every fourth year. Why not make February 29th that day?

Another way that we might profitably invest in twenty-four added hours is to see it as a milepost on our personal pilgrimage. It makes sense to see this extra day as a rest stop in our non-stop lives to reflect on where we've come from. While the campaign season every four years invites us to look ahead, the last day of February each year could easily be designated a day for looking back. It can be a day for taking stock of how God has used circumstances and people to shape the person we've become.

A friend of mine has good cause to look back each time February 29th appears on the calendar. It was on that day in 1948 that Hugh Steven had a spiritual encounter that changed the direction of his life. Entering into a personal relationship with his Creator, this seventeen-year-old employee of Woodward Stores in Vancouver began to pray for a sense of direction in his career path.

As he began to read the Scripture, Hugh discovered meaningful verses that gave him cause to trust the Object of faith. He became convinced that God would guide his future. Proverbs 3:5-6 reminded him that faith was the key to unlock doors of opportunity. *"Trust in the Lord with all your heart and lean not on your own understanding. In all your ways acknowledge Him and he will direct your paths."*

This one who found faith on February 29th found the 29th chapter of Jeremiah to be a harbinger of hope. Imagine the inner confidence Hugh embraced as his eyes focused on these words: *"I know the plans I have for you,"* declares the Lord. *"Plans to prosper you and not to harm you, plans to give hope and a future."*

Although born to a single mother and adopted as a two-year-old by an unchurched couple, Hugh became a missionary statesman traveling the world as a photojournalist and writing more than forty books. Next month he will turn ninety-three. He is currently writing his next book in addition to editing a book manuscript for a friend. How's that for a leap of faith?

This week Hugh Steven will be reflecting on a wonderful life that was set in motion on another February 29th seventy-six years ago. A life that includes a woman to whom he has been married for seventy-three years and four grown children. And I ought to know. I married his oldest child.

So, what about you? How might you make the most of the bonus day you've given this year? Consider it a rest stop on whatever journey you find yourself.

My Best Friend Billy

Sixty-five years ago I lost my two front teeth, but I gained a best friend. My dad was settling into his role as pastor of a growing church in Marysville and I was doing my best to settle into second grade. A kid named Billy Crayton lived next door to the church and attended Sunday school each week. We hit it off.

In addition to sitting together at church, Billy and I chummed on the playground at recess. We rode bikes together after school and hung out at each other's homes. Saturdays found us buying French fries from a local drive-in and eating them in a nearby park. We spent a week at Bible camp. We were almost inseparable.

And then in the summer of 1964 following sixth grade, our family moved from Marysville to Wenatchee. It was hard to say goodbye to my friends… especially Billy. Initially, we wrote letters to one another. But before long we lost touch.

As the years found me graduating college and getting married, I often wondered what became of Billy. A classmate helped me locate a mailing address for my lost friend. For a few years, we exchanged Christmas cards and photos. And then nothing. Years went by.

A few weeks ago I was sorting through a box of old Christmas cards that I'd saved from special friends. Among the stack was a card from Billy. Next to his signature was a phone number. Since so many years had passed, I had no idea if it was still a working number. I called it. It rang and rang. As I was about to hang up a man's voice answered. It was Billy!

"Do you ever come to Seattle?" I asked. He indicated that the last time he'd been in the area was more than twenty-five years ago when his dad died. *"I'm headed up in a couple weeks to visit Dad's grave and show my wife the area,"* he said. *"Perhaps we could get together!"*

I was excited at the thought of seeing my boyhood bestie after so many years. Yet when I heard the dates he'd be coming, my excitement turned to disappointment. It was the very week my wife and I would be in Southern California visiting family. But then I discovered that Wendy and I would be arriving home from Orange County a few hours before they would be leaving Seattle.

"Could we possibly meet for breakfast?" I voiced my hope. And Billy expressed his mutual desire.

It was a desire that came to pass. Two weeks after that phone call, we sat at the Denny's near the Seattle airport unpacking memories of our childhood friendship. We mused about the sixty years of life that had taken place since last we were together.

I showed him classroom photos from Liberty Elementary School in which we were both pictured. There was that photo of my dad's congregation from 1959 where the two of us stood side-by-side in the front row. With my iPhone I did a selfie video greeting and texted it to Mr. Thacker, our sixth-grade teacher, who will turn 90 years old in a few months.

Billy showed me photos of his two grown sons. I shared with him photos of my three grown daughters. For more than three hours we laughed and cried together as we caught up on so many lost years of communication.

As Billy shared with me some significant health issues he was facing, I reached for his hand and prayed for God's grace and healing touch. It was a holy moment. I was reminded of another time we had joined hands in solidarity.

When we were eleven years old, Billy and I went on an overnight hike to Mount Pilchuck with the YMCA. Although the camp organizers had arranged for plenty of food, they had not brought tents. In the middle of the frigid night, as we were drenched by the pouring rain, Billy and I held hands in an attempt to stay warm. It was a tangible expression of a friendship I had missed and upon which I once again can build.

The writer of Proverbs was right on when he wrote, *"There is a friend that sticks closer than a brother."*

Eternal Love: A Valentine Story

My mom and dad had a most amazing marriage. They were sweethearts to the end. While Hollywood romances tend to be short-lived or simply scripted for the silver screen, my folks actually had the kind of relationship pictured in the movies.

Public demonstrations of affection were not considered a taboo to my parents. It was fairly easy to spot them sharing a kiss in a crowd. After fifty-eight years of marriage, they were still holding hands as "til death do us part" became a reality.

When my dad died fifteen years ago, my mom was lost. She was not accustomed to doing life on her own. Heck, she'd never learned how to fill her car with gas. Her Prince Charming always did it for her. He was there opening the door for her and warming her cup was the coffee was brewing. Dad doted on his darling wife with devotion.

I'm sure my parents helped to keep Hallmark profitable. They gave each other greeting cards on every imaginable occasion. Birthdays, anniversaries, Christmas and Valentines Day. My dad always referred to my mom as sweetheart. And my mom always signed her cards with a kiss (imprinted with a fresh application of red lipstick).

For the eleven years my mom lived without my dad, she continued to pine for her soulmate. Although she learned to get by, she never ceased talking about the love of her life. He was her everything. It was "Edwin this" and "Edwin that." Recently I read through her diary entries near to the time her earthly journey was drawing to a close. When her mind was clouded by dementia, Mom still wrote about my dad on most every page. Even in death they were one. And when my mom passed just a few months before the pandemic, death united them once and for all.

In advance of listing with a real estate agent, my brother and I dismantled the contents of the family home Because our parents had been "collectors and savers," Marc and I recognized we had to be ruthless when it came to disposing of stuff. Countless trips were made to the Senior Center and the Goodwill. But not everything was easy to donate.

One night in the midst of emptying closets and cupboards, I came upon a rubber banded stack of love letters. They were handwritten epistles my parents had written to each other during the six months of courtship from their first date until their wedding day. There was no way I was going to toss them.

I also found shoeboxes filled with Valentines, birthday cards and anniversary cards that spanned the entire length of their marriage. Once again, I couldn't bring myself to throw them away. But what to do with them? I crammed them in a small container and placed it in the way back of my SUV. I figured I'd eventually know what to do.

As I was leaving Wenatchee for Mercer Island, I stopped at the cemetery to visit my mom and dad's grave. It was a ritual I first embraced when my dad was laid to rest in 2008. Standing over their headstone, I made note of what I saw. In addition to a laminated photo and the engraved dates of their birth and death, there were four words. Eternal love. Eternal life. As devout Christians, they believed death was the doorway to eternal life. As devoted spouses, my dad and mom were a lasting example of eternal love.

And then the thought came to me: *"Why not leave a pair of the greeting cards I'd salvaged on the grave?"* And so I did. And so I do most every time I leave Wenatchee for home. I reach into the case of cards in the back my car and leave a pair of love notes on that granite slab.

Of course, I know the wind might carry the cards away. The rain might render the inscription each contains unreadable. But that's okay. For as long as they remain on the grave, they are a tangible reminder for me (and for those who pass by) of the kind of marriage I attempt to emulate.

A Prayer for Unity in the Spirit of Dr. Seuss

This weekend marks what would have been the 120th birthday of Theodore Geisel, aka Dr. Seuss. Born in 1904, Geisel passed away in 1991 having left his imagination and creative mark on our culture. Not even the Grinch can steal our fascination and affection for this legend.

Earlier this week I dressed up in my "Cat in the Hat" costume and read books by the good doctor in area schools. That's become my annual tradition this time of the year. It's fun to see how Dr. Seuss fever fuels reading frenzy among elementary age students.

I typically read "Green Eggs and Ham" to an enthusiastic crowd of kids who often jump in and join me with "I will not eat them ANYWHERE!" This classic Seuss tale deals with forming negative opinions about certain foods before even trying them.

After reading the story in character with much flair and dramatic pauses, I can take off my hat and elaborate a bit on the bottom-line message. It has to do with ways we prejudge things and people without getting to know them. And then without actually putting anything on my gray balding head, I can put on my "preacher's hat" and call the kids to get to know those in school they aren't sure they'd like or those who are different than themselves. The fact is, once we "try" new things and get others a chance, we often end up liking them.

Another annual tradition that I observe this time of year is giving the invocation at the State Legislature. I look forward to this opportunity as much as I do my "Cat in the Hat" appearances. As I pondered what to include in my comments in Olympia, I reflected on the "Green Eggs" prejudice that often punctuates the rhetoric of red and blue states and the need for finding common causes on which politicians can agree.

The disturbing division on the political landscape prompted me to pen a prayer dealing with unity. Because my "day to pray" fell on the eve of Dr. Seuss birthday, I decided to craft my invocation in rhyme as an homage to Theodore Geisel. And so, this is what I prayed this past Friday before our lawmakers.

Dear Lord, Creator God, Most High
I ask Your help as these will try
to do their best to face the test
tho' details may be dry.

Here in the shadow of Rainier,
where long-term fixes as unclear,
we take the time with words that rhyme
to sense Your Presence here.

Please grant to these who seek to serve
all those who have been thrown a curve
the means to hear what others fear
by finding inner nerve.

And may the cost of compromise
be paid by colleagues who are wise
to what it takes to celebrate
solutions to life's whys.

So at the start of this new day,
we pause with purpose as we pray
for unity that all may see
the goals that guide our way. Amen.

Love is a Verb

I came across an old photo that I took the day my brother and I closed down the family home after my mom died. It's a picture of my folks' front door that boasted an I LOVE WENATCHEE decal. As I stared at the reflection of the front yard in the window of the door, I began to reflect on how one's love of their hometown might best be expressed.

It's not enough to just paste a bumper sticker on your car or slap a decal on a window of your home. It takes more than boasting about what you love. We have to back up our words with actions.

Last month I gave my wife a card for Valentine's Day. In it I conveyed my love for her. You most likely gave your significant other a card, a box of candy or a bouquet of flowers. That's just what we do, right? But the essence of love is not limited to traditional offerings given one day of the year. And it's not best communicated with something that can be purchased at a Hallmark store or a florist's shop.

One of my favorite books is *Love Does* by Bob Goff. In this inspiring volume, the author illustrates in fun and creative ways how actions express what we value. For this lawyer-turned-motivational speaker, love is more than an emotion. Another book that comes at the same idea from a slightly different angle is *Love is a Verb* by Gary Chapman. He's the guy who has helped countless couples navigate the twists and turns of romance with his best-selling volume *The Five Love Languages*. Both authors are convinced that we must put feet to our feelings.

When it comes to showing love for Wenatchee (or wherever you live), you can live out the slogan on a decal or bumper sticker in tangible ways. What about picking up litter when you're walking on a trail or through a parking lot. My neighbor Michael Medved is passionate about removing trash from the beautiful community where I live. As he walks to synagogue every Saturday, he carries a grabber and a garbage bag to "put litter in its place."

Showing love for your community also means supporting local businesses and not simply buying everything on Amazon. While clicking a button on your computer may be more convenient (and possibly less expensive), shopping locally is a tangible way to prove your love. Giving our independent privately-owned bookstore the business is one of the ways I make sure my civic pride is not simply lip service.

Loving your community also involves voicing your opinion at PTA meetings and public forums. It involves writing letters to the editor conveying concern for what you feel needs to be addressed to keep your community healthy. It also means finding the appropriate platform to express gratitude for those in town who are making a positive difference. At our Rotary Club, we celebrate citizens and students who mentoring others.

One of the most well-known passages in the Bible is the 13th chapter of First Corinthians. In it, the Apostle Paul describes what love looks like. The *"Love Chapter"* (as it is often called) is typically read at weddings. And while that is most appropriate, the reason it was written was to challenge church members to practice what they professed to believe. The apostle called them to show love by being patient, kind and humble. Quite simply he said that love is something you do more than something you feel (or talk about). For Saint Paul, love was a verb.

That's a great reminder for all of us. With Valentine's Day in the rearview mirror, we need to remember that expressing our affection to significant others in our lives (or voicing our love for where we live) is not limited to just one day a year. Giving a greeting card or a dozen roses on February 14th is a great tradition, but demonstrating what's behind the Valentine or the flowers is our calling continually all year long.

A Day for Patrick and Other Saints

As you read this, I will be arriving in Switzerland beginning a three-month assignment as the interim pastor of the International Church of Luzern. It is a congregation comprised of English-speaking Christ-followers from all over the world.

Those who attend the ICL are from South Africa, West Africa, Wales, New Zealand, Great Britain, the Netherlands, Germany and a variety of other countries. In many ways it's like a gathering of the United Nations. Along with a handful of others, my wife and I will represent the United States.

I find it appropriate that my very first Sunday is on Saint Patrick's Day. In recognition of those who hail from the Emerald Isle, this American clergyman will reference the patron saint of Ireland in my debut sermon.

Patrick was born into a Romanized family in Britain in the 5th century. At the age of sixteen he was kidnapped by Irish pirates who enslaved him. For six years he endured forced labor as a herdsman, but during that time his faith grew. It was during this dark season he discovered what it meant to be a shepherd of God's people.

After escaping and returning home, Patrick felt called to go back to Ireland with the message of a loving God who freed spiritual captives from lives of slavery to self.

But the essence of my first homily will focus on the fact that Patrick is not the only saint worthy of contemplation today or any other day. According to the Apostle Paul in his first century correspondence, ordinary Christ-followers are to be considered saints. The word comes from the root word that means "to sanctify" or to "set apart."

For example, Paul begins his letter to the Philippians: *"To all the saints in Christ Jesus who are in Philippi."* He viewed them as set-apart from the non-religious or worshipers of pagan gods.

Saints are more than those the Catholic church has canonized. In a very real sense, saints are all who belong to God and (like Patrick) have found their purpose in reflecting God's love. And truth be told, Saint Patrick never was actually canonized by the Church.

In addition to describing the life of Patrick in my Swiss pulpit on Sunday, I will show off a plaque one of my daughters recently gave me. Boasting a green shamrock, the message on the wooden wall hanging declares *"Tis a Wonderful Life."* Allison knows I am a fan of the movie that features the contagious generosity of George Bailey. It was the perfect Saint Patrick's gift.

And when you think about it, Frank Capra's fictional character does portray an everyday ordinary saint. He is one set-apart from the crowd in his community by a life that is distinctively different. His life was not perfect, but he definitely impacted those around him. I guess you could say George Bailey was an imperfect saint.

Speaking of imperfect saints… Several years ago, I published a volume of poetry. My intended audience was people of faith. I was primarily thinking of leaders in the church, but not just them. I titled the book "Sunday Rhymes and Reasons: Inspirational poetry to pastors, leaders and other imperfect saints."

My first Sunday in the Swiss church will also feature me introducing lyrics to an Irish song my Norwegian mother taught me when I was a kid. With the best Irish brogue I can muster, I will sing…

"Cheer up you saints o' God, there's nothing to worry about.
Nothing to make you feel afraid, nothing to make you doubt.
Remember God is over all so why not trust Him and shout.
You'll be sorry you worried at all tomorrow morning."

I smile as I think of my mom singing that little ditty. She sang it with gusto and I followed her lead. But I am also prone to smile as I think of myself challenging others to trust the Lord when I am just as imperfect as George Baileys of the world. Like them, I am prone to worry, fear and doubt. And yet as a child of God, Saint Paul indicates that I am entitled to claim the title of saint. I call that amazing grace! Don't you?

Brotherly Love and Sister Cities

Walking through the medieval town of Luzern has become a daily ritual. My wife and I are averaging five miles a day taking in all the fascinating sights. On one such recent sojourn I happened upon a half-completed mural at a pedestrian bridge leading to the walled city. Seeing the artist, I stopped to chat. To my amazement, he was an American from Chicago.

I smiled as I told Jeff Zimmermann that my wife and I had raised our three daughters in suburban Chicago. I explained why we were currently in Switzerland. He told me that he had been chosen by a committee to help commemorate the 25th anniversary of the Sister City relationship between Chicago and Luzern. Quite appropriately a bridge was identified as the "canvas" on which the artwork connecting two cities would be painted.

Together Jeff and I examined his part of the project, one wall on one side of the bridge. Since our family was living in Chicagoland during the time the two cities first "joined hands," I felt a kindred connection.

A few days later I met Marco and Vero Schmid, artists from Luzern, who were painting the wall on the other side of the bridge. Because they were influenced by time spent in Queens, New York, the duo called themselves Queen Kong. Amazingly, I discovered Marco studied with one of the teachers in the International Church where I am currently serving as the interim pastor. I, too, felt a connection to them. Seeing Marco and Vero's art celebrating Chicago on their side of the bridge brought a smile to my face.

Meeting Jeff, Marco and Vero helped me to realize that in the brief time in Luzern I have been continuously building bridges with strangers. Furthermore, it has reminded me that bridge building is a key component of my calling as a Christian pastor. And as a person of the cloth, I've come to see that bridges matter much more than walls.

For the past two decades my wife and I have lived on an island in the middle of Lake Washington. We are connected to Seattle and Bellevue by two bridges. Those bridges are our lifeline. Without them, we would be isolated and insulated. Without bridges, we would be deprived of our potential.

As I've reflected on life with bridges and life without them, I've realized that too much of my earlier life was invested in constructing walls instead of building bridges. Concerned that I would be adversely affected by values and perspectives that were at odds with my worldview, I consistently walled myself off from those who saw God and others differently than I.

Citing a verse in the Bible that talked about "coming apart from the world and being separate," I buttressed my rationale for remaining at a distance. As a result, I failed to earn the right to be taken seriously by those with whom I hoped to share my faith. In the process, I projected a "holier than thou" attitude that undermined my desires.

When I became a chaplain ten years ago, I was charged by my job description to provide spiritual nurture and care to people of various backgrounds. I began to build more bridges while dismantling bricks that separated from unnecessary walls. As I did I recognized the Pharisee-like tendencies of my youth. Gratefully, I saw how easy it was to extend a hand of friendship and love as did the first century carpenter-turned-rabbi whom I follow.

As you likely know, *phileo* is one of the Greek words for love found in the New Testament. It is a brotherly kind of love. It is the word from which Philadelphia derives its name. It is a love that esteems the value of the other. The Sister Cities concept is an attempt to intentionally build *phileo* relationships between municipalities. It is a great concept.

And to that end, I am determined to increasingly establish *phileo* friendships with those in my sphere of influence including those with whom I differ about religion, politics and culture. Care to join me?

An Easter Godwink in Switzerland

Some might call it a coincidence. I choose to call it a Godwink!

After the first of the year, my wife and I were contacted about possibly serving the International Church of Luzern in Switzerland. Their pastor had just retired and they were looking for someone like to me to provide pastoral leadership for three months until the new pastor from The Netherlands would arrive.

The opportunity was too good to pass up. In addition to seeing a new part of the world, accepting the job would allow me to do what I love. Having recently retired, I was excited to be able to preach again. And on Easter Sunday no less. After all, Easter Sunday is my very favorite occasion to lead God's people in worship. For me it's the most important day in the Christian calendar.

About the time I accepted the invitation to go to this English-speaking congregation in the Alps, something else was happening I knew nothing about. The headmaster of Whittier Christian High School in Southern California was finalizing the itinerary of a study tour in Europe for his students, staff and parents.

When Carl Martinez learned from the travel agency that his group would be in Luzern on Easter Sunday, he went on an internet search to see if there was an English-speaking congregation in the city. Upon discovering the International Church of Luzern online, he contacted the church who extended a gracious invitation to join them.

As Wendy and I prepared to leave for Switzerland, the church chairman let me know that my third Sunday in Luzern would be a rather unusual one. She indicated that the size of the congregation would likely double with a school group from the United States attending ICL for Easter worship.

When I learned the name and location of the school that would be coming, I was immediately intrigued. My wife Wendy had taught at Whittier Christian School forty-eight years ago. What were the odds that a group like that would be worshipping with us during our short stay? I couldn't help but wonder if one of the parents or faculty traveling with the group might have been a student in my wife's third grade class back in 1976.

After landing in Switzerland, I began to work on the details for Easter Sunday at ICL. I decided to Facetime with the headmaster of the Whittier School. I expressed delight that his group would be joining us to celebrate Christ's resurrection. I also indicated my wife's connection to his school. Mr. Martinez told me that although the campus at which my wife had taught had closed some years ago, it was entirely possible that one of the parents or staff from his group might have attended Wendy's school at the time.

I told Mr. Martinez that we were looking forward to having a group from Southern California with us. I related our family's connection to the area. My wife's ninety-three year old parents have lived in Orange County for over fifty years. Additionally, I told him that my wife's brother lives in Yorba Linda, California and attends the Evangelical Free Church there.

"Wait!" Mr. Martinez interrupted. "Your brother-in-law is a member of the Free Church in Yorba Linda? That's where I've attended for the past twenty years. What's his name?"

When I told Mr. Martinez my wife's brother was Dave Steven, he informed me they were part of the same men's ministry. It was simply amazing! Of all the hundreds of churches there are in Southern California, how likely would it be that this headmaster who was bringing his school group to our church in Switzerland was part of my brother-in-law's church?

Before we hang up the headmaster said, "Oh there's one more thing, Pastor Greg. You might be interested in knowing that our original itinerary had us in Stuttgart on Easter. A recent change means we'll be in Luzern."

Looking back, I discovered that the travel agent for the school group made the change in their itinerary about the time my wife and I were contacted about serving the congregation in Switzerland. He knew nothing about the church or the church's interim pastor. And how appropriate! Easter is all about unexpected turns of events that find us scratching our heads in amazement.

Easter Sunday (Take 2)

This weekend Orthodox Christians around the world are celebrating the resurrection of Jesus. Because the Orthodox Church bases its observance of Easter on the ancient Julian calendar (in contrast to the Gregorian calendar followed by Western Christians), the most holy day of Christendom is celebrated on different days. Typically, the two Easters are a week apart. This year there is more than a month separating the two observances.

As a Protestant pastor with Greek ancestral roots, I have historically celebrated both the traditional Easter with my congregations and the Orthodox Easter with my family. When I was a young boy, my dad taught me the Greek Easter greeting. And to this day our family greets one another with *"Christos anesti! Alithos anesti!"*

This year finds me celebrating both Western and Orthodox Easter in Lucerne, Switzerland. And for both occasions there is the perfect spot in town at which to sit and contemplate the cornerstone of the Christian faith.

If you have ever visited Lucerne, you likely have stopped at the Wounded Lion Monument. This amazing rock sculpture, designed by famed Danish artist Bertel Thorvaldsen, commemorates the 760 members of the Swiss Guard who lost their lives protecting the King of France during the French Revolution in 1792. The monumental effort to carve the gigantic lion in the side of a sandstone cliff began in 1819 and was completed two years later.

The lion, who measures 20 feet high and is 33 feet long, lies with a broken spear in his back and his head bowed. He is obviously dying. Mark Twain called it "the most moving and mournful piece of stone in the world."

I first saw the Lucerne Lion in-person six weeks ago while approaching Holy Week. As I stared at the beautiful (yet haunting) work of art, I couldn't help but think of the Christ-like figure in the first of C. S. Lewis' Chronicles of Narnia.

In "The Lion, the Witch and the Wardrobe," the first of Lewis' chronicles, Aslan the lion willingly lays down his life to lift the curse that has held the Kingdom of Narnia captive. The lion's lifeless body lies cold and still on a giant stone table.

Using his palette of language, C. S. Lewis paints an unforgettable picture that conjures up the events of Good Friday. This gifted wordsmith conveys the suffering that provides the backdrop for the glorious message of the resurrection.

In his book as the symbolic story unfolds, Lewis pictures Easter Sunday as well. The stone table is discovered by the children without any sign of Aslan. They soon encounter the lion fully alive. Aslan has returned from the dead. The children also realize that Narnia has returned to its original glory.

The land that had been labeled *"as always winter but never Christmas"* was once again blooming in springtime glory. The visible and invisible evidence of Immanuel (God-with-us) provided Narnia with proof of a redeemed kingdom.

Although I have long believed that the truth of Easter is an ongoing reality and not simply a single day on the liturgical calendar, this year it is all the more in focus. With the two Easter observances of the

Christian Church being more than a month apart, there is cause to contemplate the fact the resurrection can be celebrated continuously.

If you're like me, hardly a week goes by without learning of someone you know (or know of) who has passed away. Death dominates the landscape of our lives. The shadow of sorrow creeps across our hopes and dreams. Grief is an ever-present reality. Parents die. Spouses receive a terminal diagnosis. Siblings leave us prematurely. Even our children are not exempt.

And given the grim reality of the Grim Reaper's unsolicited visits to our families, knowing that death has been defeated once and for all is something I can't celebrate enough. Having two Easters is just fine. In fact, I would welcome even a few more. *Christ is risen! He is risen indeed!*

A Somber Anniversary

This weekend marks the 112th anniversary of the day that most famous of all ships carried 1,522 people to their watery graves. Did you know that the Titanic was three football fields long? She was 11 stories tall and 92 feet wide. The infamous ship tipped the scales at 46,000 tons.

At the time, she was the largest and most luxurious ship ever built. This vessel "fit for a king" could carry nearly 3,000 passengers and crew. She had her own swimming pools, suites, restaurants, Turkish baths and squash courts. There was even a Parisian sidewalk café complete with strolling musicians.

With sixteen water-tight compartments below sea level, the Titanic was deemed unsinkable. The 14,000 workers at Harland and Wolff Shipbuilders in Belfast spent thirty-six months assembling this beautiful craft. They took pride in the fact that she was the most seaworthy vessel ever constructed.

The Titanic was the pride of the White Star Line. Perhaps it was the belief that this vessel was so seaworthy that there were less than half the number of recommended lifeboats installed. No one could imagine a situation in which every passenger and crew member would need one.

With a sense of his own pride, Captain Edward Smith was determined to complete the journey from England to New York in record time. Since the maiden voyage of the Titanic would be his last before retiring, he had this one last opportunity to achieve his desired legacy and line his pockets.

To achieve his goal, Captain Smith knew he would have to move his vessel at 26 knots day and night in order to arrive in New York's harbor in six days. His pride trumped prudence.

On the evening of April 14, 1912, the Titanic struck an iceberg and was swallowed up in the frigid waters of the North Atlantic. The ship "not even God could sink" sank. Only 706 lived to tell of the unthinkable nightmare.

One of those who perished was a thirty-nine year old British pastor by the name of John Harper. Reverend Harper was a widower enroute to Chicago to become the next pastor of the historic Moody Memorial Church. Traveling with his six-year-old daughter and his niece, Harper's status as a parent and guardian entitled him to a seat on a lifeboat (on which his loved ones would eventually be rescued). But this man of faith willingly gave up his seat. His concern was sharing his faith with those for whom there would not be enough lifeboats.

A sailor, who was one of the last to be rescued from the sinking vessel, later attested to the fact that it was Harper who asked the band leader on the deck to play *Nearer My God to Thee*. While the musicians played a somber soundtrack to the real-life drama playing out on the Atlantic, Harper gathered a large group of people around him. He knelt in the center of the circle and prayed on behalf of those who were nearer to God than they ever imagined they would be when the ship left England. Soon they drowned.

The pride of the ship's captain and the humility of the reverend is most noteworthy. The contrast was engraved in my heart some years ago when my eye caught sight of a little book in a thrift store. The beautiful volume contained illustrated lyrics to *Nearer My God to Thee*, a hymn that will always be associated with the sinking of the Titanic.

I carefully opened the fragile book. What I read gave me pause. This printed treasure was inscribed to a young man by the name of Francis

Griset by his grandmother. The occasion was the boy's 8th birthday. It was dated July 14, 1911. Amazing! The book was given exactly nine months before that hymn would be played as the ship was sinking.

This weekend while we ponder the tragic circumstances of the Titanic, why not reflect on the "icebergs" in your life that could capsize your dreams? As with Captain Smith, the lust for power, popularity and wealth puts us on a collision course with pride, arrogance and failure.

We might think we are unsinkable, but as a bumper sticker I once saw aptly suggests *"Don't believe everything you think!"*

An Invitation to Number Our Days

This week I reach a milestone. My birthday cake is entitled to seventy-two candles. But given our corporate concern for global warming, my wife will likely only light one solitary wax sentry. And that's okay. Too many miniature flames make for too much light that in turn exposes too little hair and too many wrinkles.

Given a temporary work assignment in Switzerland, this is the first birthday in those seventy-two years in which I will celebrate outside of the United States. And truth be told, this opportunity to serve an English-speaking church in Luzern for three months is the best birthday present I could have asked for. Curiously, thirty-six years ago my wife and I found ourselves in a similar situation. I was asked to take a temporary assignment in Nome, Alaska. Taking a leave of absence from my congregation in California, I worked for a missionary radio station for a couple months.

Like my current assignment as interim pastor of the International Church of Luzern, working for KICY radio was an unforgettable opportunity to meet new people and explore new parts of God's green earth for the very first time. And to think that our Alaskan adventure was almost exactly half my life ago! Where has the time gone? That summer assignment in Nome seems but a few short years ago. Mindboggling to be sure!

The Hebrew psalmist declares *"Man is like a breath. His days are like a passing shadow."* (Psalm 144:4) St. James put it this way, *"What is your life? For you are a mist that appears for a little time and then vanishes."* (James 4:14)

Like a summer day in the Pacific Northwest, 72 seems like the perfect number. Not too hot. Not too cold. It's just about perfect. But for me it also comes with the candid realization that my days are numbered. If I live as long as my dad did, I only have ten years left. If I live to celebrate the same number of birthdays my mom had, I have just twenty years left.

Speaking of my precious little mom, when it came to birthdays and acknowledging how old she was, she had a signature saying for which she was known. *"Age is just a number. And mine is unlisted!"* Or like the poster I hung on the wall in my college dorm room *"Today is the first day of the rest of your life."* Wow! Was that really fifty-four years ago? As a freshman I wanted to make every day count. And all these years later, I still do.

Birthdays are an annual occasion to give yourself permission to take stock of the speed at which time flies. In other words, they are an opportunity for "give and take." Give heed to choices that today offers and take time to evaluate which ones you will choose. Give up trying to undo the past and take control of your future. Give God thanks for achievements you've accomplished thus far on life's journey and take a break to bask in His many blessings.

I'm blown away by the goodness of a Creator who allowed me over the past seventy-two years to meet such incredible people, travel to such fascinating places, do such a variety of jobs in addition to sharing my wonderful life with my beautiful wife for forty-two years and raising three amazing daughters. But I know I am not alone. As you look back on your life to date, you no doubt have blessings too numerous to number as well.

In the only psalm that Moses ever wrote, the Prince of Egypt poignantly prays *"Lord, teach us to number our days that we might gain a heart of wisdom."* (Psalm 90:12) It doesn't take a math major to count our blessings and number our days. It just takes someone who recognizes the bottom line of maximizing one's life.

Learning to Say Learning to Say *Grüezi*

Within a few days our twelve weeks in Switzerland will come to an end. And once again I have been reminded how quickly time passes. As St. James informs us in his letter in the New Testament, *"Life is a vapor."* Or as the Steve Miller Band puts it, *"Time keeps on slippin' into the future."*

At any rate, our time here in the land of Heidi, chocolate and watches wasn't long enough to learn many words in Swiss German (the dialect spoken in Luzern). By their own admission, those who live here say Schweizerdeutsch is quite different from high German. It's quite difficult to master.

I was grateful that the International Church of Luzern was an English-speaking congregation. But Wendy and I did learn how to say *hello* in Swiss German. When we arrived at our apartment in the middle of March, we were greeted by a white sign with red letters on a shelf in the entry way. Attempting to sound out grüezi, I asked how to say this seemingly unpronounceable word. I also asked what it meant.

"It's pronounced *GRIT-see*," the chair of the pastoral search committee explained. "It's how we greet one another. And it's not all that difficult to say."

Almost immediately Wendy and I began saying grüezi as we'd meet people in the store and on the street. To our delight strangers greeted us with grüezi in return. We said grüezi often as we took time to visit in the homes of our Swiss congregation. We'd say grüezi as we took day trips on the lake or to the mountains with the members. We'd say grüezi as we'd study the Bible together in small groups.

Learning to say hello to this church family has been deeply rewarding. As the interim minister I was able to give myself fully to loving the flock without being burdened with the demands normally associated with a full-time call. It's the kind of assignment I've come to appreciate.

I've served in the role of interim pastor twice in my forty-five years in ministry. Both situations were most fulfilling. In each case, I was tasked with the challenge of holding the congregation together while they anticipated their next fulltime shepherd.

But one of the hard parts of being an interim pastor is making new friendships and investing in relationships only to have to say goodbye a short time later. If you're wired the way I am, you don't hold people at arm's length in order to avoid the pain that goes with farewells. Pastors like me can't help drawing close to those around you and making memories together. It's just what we do. But then comes the grief. Or as Shakespeare put it, *"Parting is such sweet sorrow."*

I first learned the emotional letdown of saying goodbye to new friends while working my way through seminary. My summer job for three years found me escorting tour groups to Alaska and through the Canadian Rockies. Over a two-week period, I'd get to know my passengers in a very personal way. In a relatively short period of time, we'd share family history and hopes for our future while experiencing memorable moments together that will last a lifetime.

And then I would be forced to say goodbye to new friends. I went into a bit of a depression. The grief was real. The sadness was palatable. But in retrospect, I would call it *good grief*. I was grieving because I had experienced genuine joy and meaningful friendship before having to say goodbye.

As I come to the end of this Swiss ministry adventure, I'm once again experiencing *good grief*. The pain is real but so are the connections that Wendy and I have made. Friendships have been born that will be lasting. Relationships have been established that were mutually beneficial. Learning how to say *hi* in the language of the locals came with a windfall in spite of the tears. But I'm not sorry for the sorrow.

It's inevitable. Hellos always give way to goodbyes. The present eventually becomes the past. The door of opportunity swings open and shut. But in it all, learning to say grüezi (in any language) is the key that unlocks the doors God places in our path.

In the Shadow of the Mountain

Switzerland is known for its snowcapped mountains, emerald-green hillsides and bell-bedecked bovines. If you've ever traveled to the land of Heidi, you likely have visited Luzern. It is the most popular tourist destination in Switzerland.

And for those who visit this medieval city, three memorable landmarks distinguish it. There is the Wounded Lion Monument that I referenced in my column last week. There is the covered wooden bridge with adjacent water tower build in the 1300s. And there is magnificent Mount Pilatus that dominates the skyline. Tourists take photos and a cable-car to the top of this majestic summit.

While serving the International Church of Luzern in Switzerland, my wife and I are staying in a third-floor apartment above the sanctuary. The view we have of Mount Pilatus from our living room window is stunning.

As I look out at Mount Pilatus each morning, I'm reminded of one of my favorite passages in the Old Testament. Psalm 121 is one of the psalms of ascent. It is part of a grouping of songs that the people of God would sing as they made their way to Jerusalem for the three major festivals. The psalm finds the psalmist focused on the Judean hills that surround the city of Jerusalem.

In the old King James Version of the Bible, the first verse of the psalm suggests that the dominating hills represent a source of security and comfort. *"I lift up mine eyes to the hills from whence cometh my help..."*

But such a translation of the Hebrew text into English is not a very accurate one. A better rendering would be as follows: "I lift up my eyes to the hills! Where will my help come from?" In other words, the hills represent a cause for concern. The overshadowing elevation that envelops the faithful (as they make their pilgrimage to the City of David) underscores their vulnerability.

In 1997 when Wenatchee High School presented me with the Alumnus of the Year Award, I was called on to make a speech as part of the commencement ceremonies.

My talk included memories I had of growing up on Gellatly Street at the base of Saddle Rock Mountain. Our home was just a stone's throw from the old Apple-atchee Stables and Riders Club where the current high school now stands.

In my remarks I also made reference to Psalm 121. Calling attention to the recognizable peak perched above our alma mater, I invited the students to think of Saddle Rock Mountain as a metaphor for the challenges they will face as they move ahead in life.

On a night filled with thoughts of after-graduation parties, autographing yearbooks and time with out-of-town relatives, I'm fairly certain my comments about looming obstacles in the future fell on deaf ears. What big issues yet to be revealed in their lives could they possibly be thinking about?

But those same individuals, who were capped and gowned twenty-seven years ago, know all too well the heights of challenges that now dwarf them. Worries over health, employment, the economy, marriage, divorce, addictions and death. There are the challenges of raising their own children and providing a quality education for them.

Saddle Rock Mountain and Mount Pilatus each provide a visual aid to the simple truth I'm attempting to convey. The monumental problems that loom in the distance invite us to look beyond them to a God who knows the solution.

I take confidence that within a page or two of Psalm 121 in my Bible is Psalm 125. I consider these two companion psalms. Both ancient pieces of poetry speak of mountains that symbolize problems. And both look to the Lord as the One on whom our focus should be.

"As the mountains surround Jerusalem, so the LORD surrounds his people both now and forevermore…" Psalm 125:2

Oh, The People You Will Meet

One of my favorite Dr. Seuss books is *"Oh, the Places You Will Go."* I first heard it read at my oldest daughter's high school baccalaureate service. In the good doctor's inimitable way, Theodore Seuss Geisel (did you know that Seuss was his middle name?) offers a prescription for life. He paints a word picture of endless possibilities as one faces the future.

It's a book for those just graduating high school and those who've been out for half a century. When I retired ten months ago, I had no clue that one of the places my wife and I would go for three months would be Luzern, Switzerland. But there we went and here we are for a couple more weeks.

During our time in central Switzerland, I've met a multitude of marvelous people. Many of those notable new friends members of the International Church of Luzern, but not all. While climbing a watchtower on the medieval wall in the old city, I encountered three young people dressed in Mennonite clothing. When I heard them speak English, I was surprised. Since most everyone in this area speaks German or Swiss German, to hear my own language spoken was cause for pause. I asked where they were from.

"America!" they offered. "But where exactly ?" I pressed. "About an hour south of Seattle, Washington!" they replied. I couldn't believe it!

I met another couple of tourists in the historical museum in the newer part of Luzern. Once again, when I heard them speaking English, I asked where they were from. They told me they were from Central Washington. When I told them I grew up in Wenatchee, they told me they had raised their kids in Pateros. Again, I was amazed.

And then a few weeks ago, when my daughters from Seattle arrived for a visit, I was in the tourist information office to arrange for a boat ride on Lake Luzern. I heard the persons in front of me speaking English. I inquired as to where home was for them. They told me San Jose. When I told them I was from the Seattle area, their eyes widened at they said they vacationed each summer in Wenatchee and Lake Chelan. I smiled as I told them I grew up in Wenatchee and that we have a summer cabin in Chelan.

They introduced themselves as Jerry and Pam Huss. As our conversation continued, the couple told me they were good friends of Bart and Sheila Clennons, Mike and Joanne Walker and Don and Kit McArthur. Although I didn't recognize those names initially, Jan indicated that Sheila Clennon's father had been a doctor in the valley. When I asked his name, she told me it was Dr. Hildebrand, I smiled. Sheila's dad had been one of my mom's doctors.

Later in the day when I went back to our apartment, I looked up Sheila Hildebrand on the internet. To my surprise I discovered she'd been an Apple Blossom Festival princess in 1964. That was the year our family moved to Wenatchee sixty years ago.

As I attempted to find Bart and Sheila on Facebook, I realized it was the start of Apple Blossom Festival Weekend. What a fun discovery! And before the weekend was over, I'd successfully informed the Clennons of my serendipitous encounter with their dear friends halfway around the world.

Not all the people I've met in the past three months have come with such coincidental nuances. But meeting people in Switzerland from all around the world has filled my journal with all kinds of wonderful anecdotes. I've been reminded that there really aren't strangers in our lives. Just friends we haven't yet met.

God is Now Here

About the time I was contacted by the International Church in Luzern to consider becoming their interim pastor, my wife and I were reading a book by my friend Mark Batterson. In it, Mark called attention to a quote that the late Swiss psychiatrist Carl Jung had inscribed on the entrance to his home in Zurich. In Latin it reads *"Vocatus atque non vocatus deus aderit."* The translation is *"Called or not called God is present."*

According to Jung, he had the quotation engraved in stone above his front door to remind his patients and himself that *"the fear of the Lord is the beginning of wisdom."*

When I read the quote and recognized the connection to Switzerland, I thought it would be the perfect saying to have displayed in the entry way of our apartment in Luzern. Searching the internet, I found the quote in an attractive font and printed it out. A visit to our local thrift store on Mercer Island resulted in finding the ideal frame in which to place the slogan.

For the past two months the quote Carl Jung cherished has greeted our guests. And since being here in Switzerland, I've learned that Jung's grave marker also includes the Latin affirmation. Those six little words deeply impacted his perspective of life (and death).

Upon further research I discovered that Jung came across this Latin slogan in the 1563 writings of Erasmus. But the original quote can be traced back over two thousand years. It was supposedly delivered as Delphic oracle in Greece when the Lacedemonians were pondering an attack on Athens. That little piece of trivia piqued my interest in that my paternal grandfather was born and raised near Delphi in Greece.

But regardless of the origin of the phrase, what matters most is the truth of the saying. I have come to value its meaning. It is a simple affirmation that calls to mind the presence of the Almighty all the time everywhere whether we are aware of it or not.

Both Judaism and Christianity affirm the omnipresence of God. Psalm 139, for example, is an artistic portrait painted with words celebrating the beauty of this reality. There is no escaping God's presence. We live our lives in the companionship of our Creator. It's a truth whose consequences recently came into focus for me.

Before retiring as the chaplain at Covenant Living at the Shores on Mercer Island last summer, I helped lead a ministry called BeFrienders. This unique program provides extensive training for residents in therapeutic non-judgmental listening skills. Upon completion of the various modules, this team of trained "listeners" is able to extend the pastoral care provided by the chaplain's office. The BeFrienders were a real boon to my ministry.

One of the core values of the BeFrienders program is *"Caring not curing."* Such an affirmation freed the trained listeners with whom I worked to simply be attentive to their assigned client and hear their heart.

Another core value of BeFrienders is *"God is always present."* I especially resonated with that. Not only does it mirror Jung's slogan, it freed my team to come alongside their clients assuming the Lord was already involved in the situation. And knowing that God is present, no challenge, problem or emotional pain was beyond healing. Such a truth was both liberating and faith-producing. If God is present, so also is hope.

Long before I became aware of Carl Jung's Latin slogan, I saw a bumper sticker that called attention to the omniscience of God. Without any spaces the following words were displayed on the back of a sedan. As I focused on the bumper, I read **GODISNOWHERE**.

Initially it looked as if the phrase was implying that GOD IS NO WHERE. But as I looked more carefully at the words that were in bolder print, I saw that it was stating quite emphatically that GOD IS NOW HERE.

And even though it's too late to ask him personally, I can say with confidence the noted Swiss psychiatrist would agree.

Finding Common Ground

For the past three months I had the privilege of serving as the interim pastor of the International Church of Lucerne Switzerland. Members of that ecumenical English-speaking congregation are from Singapore, Indonesia, South Africa, Brazil, Columbia, Ireland, Slovakia, Hungary, Ukraine, England, France, Italy, Canada, Switzerland as well as the United States. Each Sunday as I stood before the diverse group to give my sermon, there was a sense of universal community.

While in Lucerne, I found myself repeatedly visiting the famous wounded lion monument. This amazing sculpture was carved into a sandstone cliff more than two hundred years ago. It commemorates the seven hundred Swiss Guard who lost their lives attempting to protect the king of France in 1792. The lion, who measures 20 feet high and is 33 feet long, lies with a broken spear in his back and his head bowed. He is obviously dying. Mark Twain called it "the most moving and mournful piece of stone in the world."

The haunting beauty of this magnificent work of art drew me again and again in the middle of the day to the garden-like setting in the middle of the city. There is no admission fee and it is open to the public. And believe me, the public visits big time.

In addition to taking photos and writing in my journal, I would sit on a bench and simply observe the reactions of busloads of tourists. There was almost a steady stream of "lion hunters" throughout the day. The amazement on faces as they behold the beast for the first time was noteworthy. Visitors with smartphones in hand would take multiple pictures of the lion from various vantage points. They would also take selfies with the sculpture in the background.

I noted tour groups from India, Japan, China, Scandinavia, the United Kingdom and various countries of Europe. The diverse languages spoken reminded me of the nations represented in the church I was serving. Yet, in spite of the diversity, there was a sense of unity. The magnificent sculpture provided common ground. There was harmony and oneness. That carved piece of stone pictured the peace for which we all long.

The day before my wife and I flew home to Seattle, we paid one last visit to the lion. Two college-age guys were helping an elderly man navigate the stairs in front of the monument. I engaged them in conversation. They described the joy they were experiencing helping their ninety-year-old grandfather from Virginia discover his Swiss roots. Like others I'd witnessed over the previous several weeks, they were transfixed by what they saw. Standing with their rather feeble grandfather, they posed with the others around them taking picture after picture. The lion became the great equalizer.

When I mentioned to them that I was from the Seattle area, a female tourist within earshot walked by and said, *"I'm from Poulsbo!"* To which I responded, *"Let's hear it for Sluy's Bakery!"*

I attempted to follow the ball-capped woman into the crowd. I wanted to chat about her visit to Lucerne and see if perhaps we had mutual friends in Kitsap County. But alas, she disappeared into the mass of people headed for their buses. I wish I'd gotten her name.

Although Wendy and I are now back home, the eyes of the world are focused on where we've been. This weekend at Burgenstock a mountain resort above Lake Lucerne in Central Switzerland, representatives from a multitude of nations are gathering.

The purpose of the gathering is to discuss ways to end the bloodshed in Ukraine. Although Russia and China will not be participating, there will be others dialoging determined to find solutions to global conflicts. They will look for common ground on which to build bridges to isolated islands. It is a chance for those of who can only follow developments in the media, to pray for the process taking place.

Time limitations and security precautions will likely prevent the participants from visiting the lion monument less than a half-hour away. And that is a shame. A visit to the monument would allow global leaders the chance to see what coming together looks like. It would give those who can make a difference a peek at how nations are united when they gather on common ground.

Being Alert to the World Around You

At the end of a three-month assignment in Switzerland, my wife and I spent a weekend in Paris. On Sunday we worshipped at the American Church on the Seine River near the Eiffel Tower. It was a glorious experience as Christians from various parts of the globe gathered in this century-old gothic building. A black gospel choir guided our praise. The sermon was from a South Korean woman. The stained-glass windows celebrated the universality of the Christian message.

As I left the church, I was inspired by Pastor Paik's take-away message. She invited us to celebrate and live into our artistic passions. Taking photos is one of my passions. And what better place to take pictures than in Paris. I gave myself permission to look for unique scenes to photograph.

The Pont Alexandre III called to me. Of the many bridges that span the Seine, it is the most ornate. It connects the Champs-Élysées quarter with those of the Invalides and Eiffel Tower. At one end of the bridge, I looked up and just happened to see a cherub holding a trident. It reminded me of our Seattle Mariners' whose season is off to a brilliant start. I aimed my iPhone at the figure with thoughts of sending the photo to my buddy Rick Rizzs who is the Mariners' play-by-play announcer.

Walking the length of the bridge, I made note of the grandstands being set up for the upcoming Olympic Games. I continued my trek knowing that there were large statues of Winston Churchill and Charles de Gaulle on the other side of the river. As I reached the end of the bridge, I saw a short man with long spirally hair standing at the guard rail looking over the Seine. It looked like someone from Seattle. Could it be? Here in Paris? Was it really? "Kenny!" I called out.

And Kenny G turned toward me and asked my name. We had a brief conversation. I told him we lived on Mercer Island. I explained I'd played sax up through college and then quit. He thanked me for giving it up. With a smile, he said I might have given him competition. Small chance.

After agreeing to pose for a selfie, Kenny reminded me that he still performs at Jazz Alley in Seattle between Christmas and New Year's each December.

I continued across the bridge to take a close up of Winston and Charles before hurrying back to where my wife was waiting. "Look who I just met," I said with a smile as I showed Wendy the photo on my phone. She recognized him immediately.

When I posted the photo of Kenny G on my Facebook page, those who know me weren't all that surprised. Seems I have a reputation for running into famous people quite often. But I'm convinced it doesn't have to do with who I am. Rather, I believe it has to do with simply being aware of my surroundings.

In Proverbs 20:12 we read these words... *"The hearing ear and the seeing eye, the LORD has made them both."* In other words, God has given us the ability to be aware in order that we might be alert to life through what we hear and what we see. Through our ears and our eyes we have the means to absorb people and things worth noticing.

While Wendy and I first arrived in Switzerland, our hosts told us to look up as we walked through the medieval town of Luzern. They didn't want us to miss the nuances of artistic expression that most people miss by only looking forward. I'm so glad we were given that advice. The beauty we beheld by looking up was breathtaking.

I'm reminded of that line from a poem by Elizabeth Barrett Browning. *"Earth's crammed with heaven, and every common bush afire with God: But only he who sees, takes off his shoes, The rest sit round it, and pluck blackberries and daub their natural faces unaware..."*

I don't know about you, but I for one do not want to be a blackberry picker. I want to hear the music and see the beauty of serendipities that God has hidden for us to discover (including musicians like Kenny G).

Reflections on a Fifty-Year Reunion

This weekend my wife and I will be attending our 50th class reunion at Seattle Pacific University. It will be a weekend in which we celebrate memories of the past. Although we met as freshmen on the Queen Anne Hill campus in 1970, Wendy and I weren't romantically involved during college. As a matter of fact, we dated each other's roommates.

It would be several years later when Wendy and I would rediscover one another. She was teaching elementary school in Southern California and I was a pastor in Seattle. And speaking of celebrating the past, just last week we toasted our 42nd wedding anniversary in Switzerland by attending a performance of the Vienna Symphonic Orchestra.

Returning to Seattle Pacific this weekend will trigger special memories. During our reunion dinner, I'll be emceeing the program. One of my tasks will be interviewing former classmates including the guy who beat me by twenty-eight votes to be elected student body president. Stephan Coonrod went on to have a distinguished career as a lawyer with a prominent Seattle firm.

A highlight of the evening will be the screening of a video greeting by Dr. David McKenna, who was president of SPU when we were students. President McKenna's wife Janet was actually part of our graduating class (having returned to college to complete her degree after being a stay-at-home mom).

Now at ninety-five years of age, Dr. McKenna remains active living independently with his wife of seventy-four years. He is currently completing the second volume of his memoir. He remains a mentor to me and communes with me regularly as we share a cup of Pike Place roast at his local St. Arbucks in Kirkland.

As I anticipate watching Dr. McKenna's greeting, I'm thinking back to the night of graduation in 1974 at the Seattle Opera House. There was a very special moment when our beloved president presented his wife her diploma and then proceeded to kiss her. The audience broke into spontaneous applause.

I have other memories of that memorable night where my classmates and I walked across the stage to receive our degrees. As the class clown approached the presiding dean, Tic was wearing a top hat instead of a mortar board. And in place of academic cords, he wore strands of cotton rope.

When it was Ron's turn to claim his certificate of achievement, the dean announced his name... *"Ronald Long, cum laude dah."* The audience burst into laughter.

A moment equally as funny occurred when I approached the center of the stage as my name was called by the dean. Dr. Rearick was so nervous about pronouncing my last name correctly, he called me George instead of Greg. By George, he really did!

That memorable night half a century ago found The Honorable Anne Armstrong addressing our class. She was the first women to serve as counselor to a sitting President. As a follower of Jesus, she challenged us to live out our faith with confidence in the vocations we would embrace. The evening concluded with my dad giving the benediction and asking God's blessing on the lives of those who were celebrating this rite of passage.

In the half century that has passed, so much has occurred in the lives of the Class of 1974. There have been marriages, births, divorces, changes of jobs and deaths. In fact, a special segment of our reunion will feature names and photos of deceased classmates.

Still as I think of that moment fifty years ago when Dr. McKenna kissed his wife to punctuate that magnificent milestone in her life, I think of a book by the late Methodist pastor Robert Raines. It invites us to face the present while reflecting on the past.

In "To Kiss the Joy," the author wrote, "*God sets us free to taste eternity in an hour—to create the marvelous by contagion— to notice the butterfly when it lands on your shoulder— to have the courage, to once live in unison with your dreams — and the hope, always the hope, to kiss the joy as it flies.*"

Even at the age of seventy-two or ninety-five, we are capable of demonstrating that kind of affection as we embrace life.

Oh, the Places You'll Go

A few weeks ago I made reference to the *Dr. Suess' Oh, the Places You'll Go*, a book often given to students at graduations. Having recently attended my 50-year college reunion, I'm contemplating that book title. Life is indeed a journey punctuated by an unpredictable itinerary. Had Dr. Suess' class volume been available in 1974, it would have been the perfect gift for my parents to give me. But alas, it wouldn't be written for another sixteen years.

What my dad and mom actually gave me when I graduated from Seattle Pacific was a most unusual gift. It was an Ameripass. Remember those? An Ameripass was a Greyhound bus ticket that allowed you to travel anywhere in the United States for a month. Because of my sense of adventure, it was the perfect present. And so I wouldn't have to travel alone, my folks also bought an Ameripass for my brother.

On a hot June day in 1974 Marc and I boarded an eastbound bus at the Wenatchee Greyhound depot on Mission Street. We had no set itinerary. Our goal was to cover the perimeter of the country in thirty days. Had I known on day one all that we would do and all the people we would meet, I could have written my version of *Oh, the Places You'll Go!*

It was an amazing trip. Even though it's been fifty years, it seems like only yesterday. I had the best hamburger ever at a hotel coffee shop in

Miles City, Montana. We saved money by sleeping on the bus as it continued its journey eastward. We made a quick stop for dinner at a cheap steakhouse in Chicago. We took pictures of Niagara Falls in Upstate New York. Manhattan provided us a chance to see a Broadway show in which Marlo Thomas performed. In Boston Marc and I were denied a motel room with a double bed because the manager assumed we were gay.

In Philadelphia, in addition to viewing the historical sites, my brother and I sat in the studio audience of The Mike Douglas Show. That same day we met Joe Frazier at the taping of another television show. In Washington DC we walked all 896 steps to the top of the Washington Monument. We were also treated to ice cream bars and a personal tour of the U.S. Capitol and the White House by Gerald Frank (Senator Mark Hatfield's personal aide who I had met a year earlier at SPU).

Following a stretch on Interstate 95 to Florida to visit Meredith and Rosalind Nelson (longtime Wenatchee residents who had relocated to Lakeland), our journey westward included stops in all the southern states. A highlight, before ending our trip in Hollywood, was seeing the Osmond Family perform at a casino in Las Vegas. And to think it all began at the Greyhound depot in Wenatchee.

As I contemplate that unforgettable bus trip half a century ago, I realize that every journey in our lives has a starting point. My life as a follower of Jesus can be traced to walking the center aisle on a Sunday night at my dad's church in Marysville when I was six years old. My call to ministry evolved as I preached my first sermon at the First Assembly of God Church in Wenatchee the summer of 1968. The ease I feel behind a microphone began at KPQ radio where I worked as an announcer during my senior year of high school. For my wife and me, our life together as a couple commenced at the altar of Trinity United Presbyterian Church in Santa Ana, California forty-two years ago last month.

Every journey in life has a starting point. And that includes the journeys on which we are about to embark this summer. They may not be road trips or relational adventures. They could be educational excursions that result in learning a new language or completing a requirement related to one's work.

For some they will be inward journeys of self-discovery. For my friends who have discovered freedom from self-destructive addictions, the journey of emancipation began with the first of twelve steps.

Regardless of what journey awaits us, what matters most is a starting point. And for all of us that starting point is the moment at hand. After all, today is the first day of the rest of our lives.

An Invitation to Live Like Jesus

Perhaps you read in the Wenatchee World a couple weeks ago that Martin Luther King, Jr. had a different name when he was born 95 years ago. It's true. Michael King, Jr. was named after his pastor-father Rev. Michael King, Sr.

In 1934 when young Michael was five years old, his dad, a pastor in Atlanta, attended a Baptist World Alliance gathering in Germany. While traveling through much of the country where Martin Luther ministered in the 16th century, The Reverend King was moved by Luther's impact. Upon returning to his home in Georgia, he decided to change his name (and his son's name) to honor the Protestant reformer's life.

But the name change proved to be more than simply an homage. As history would show, both men leaned into Luther's legacy and pursued the reformer's passion for justice and righteousness. For them, justice and righteousness did not mean cleaning house in a corrupt religious system. Rather it meant challenging a segregated country where racism and prejudice ran rampant. Being called by a name that called to mind courage and influence motivated both father and son to make their lives matter.

I know all about the concept of changing names. This year marks the fifty-fifth year since our family changed its name. On August 13, 1969 my dad, mom, brother and I entered the Chelan County Courthouse as the Smith family and left as the Asimakoupoulos family.

When fifteen-year-old Haralambos Asimakoupoulos arrived in this country in 1906, he wanted to be an American and so he became Harry Smith. The American-sounding surname my Greek immigrant grandfather chose was he way of parading his pride in his new homeland.

For my father, however, Smith seemed like an alias. The more my dad researched his ethnic ancestry, the more he identified with his roots. The more he longed to reclaim the original family name.

And so as I was about to begin my senior year at Wenatchee High School, I had a new identity. Greg Smith was now Greg Asimakoupoulos. And over the past fifty-five years I have celebrated the fact that I am related to those who first gave the world democracy.

Speaking of identity alterations. The Bible is replete with examples of name changes. Abram became Abraham. Sarai became Sarah. Jacob became Israel. Hadassah became Esther. Saul became Paul. And most notably, Simon became Peter.

When Jesus began referring to Simon as Peter, something happened. The fisherman-turned-disciple began to act differently. As time went on, Simon leaned into his new identity as Peter and exhibited personality qualities that were much more solid and dependable. This one who had been an unpredictable pebble in Jesus' sandal cemented his calling as a foundation stone on which the first century church would be established.

"You are Peter (in Greek "Petros" means a large boulder)" Jesus said. "And on this rock, I will build my church." His new name empowered him to become the man whose life would leave an amazing legacy.

So what is your name? My parents named me Gregory. They named my brother Marc. My wife and I named our daughters Kristin, Allison and Lauren. My daughter named her daughters Imogen and Ivy.

Did you know that some refer to their first name as their "Christian" name? Even though our first names are given us at birth, in some religious circles those names are not formalized until they are publicly verbalized through christening, baptism or dedication in church. And thus they become our "Christian" name.

In light of that, I actually had a "Christian" name before I understood what it meant to be a follower of Jesus. But when I chose to embrace His teachings. I was given a new name. I became known as a Christian (which literally means "little Christ"). And with that new name I was invited to live into the qualities ordinarily associated with Jesus. Qualities like loving, patient, empathetic, courageous, merciful, self-denying and forgiving.

As I look back at Martin Luther King, Jr. and see how his new name motivated him to live like Luther, I am challenged to not only call myself a Christian, but to live like one.

I Lift Up My Eyes to the Hills

There is a large calligraphy of Psalm 121 in a frame that belonged to my great-grandparents hanging in the entry way of our home. The parchment was given to me forty years ago when I was called as pastor to my very first congregation. It is one of my favorite psalms.

"I will lift up mine eyes unto the hills from whence cometh my help!"

But the King James Version of this familiar Scripture is not a good translation. A much better rendering of the Hebrew text is closer to this: *"I lift up my eyes to the hills! Where will my help come from?"*

The elevation of ancient Jerusalem found the psalmist looking up at a range of hills that dominated the landscape. He was surrounded by imposing summits that rendered him vulnerable to sneak attacks from his enemies. Recognizing his plight, he looked beyond the hills to the only One who could protect him.

I think about Psalm 121 as I picture the illuminated cross perched atop a hill in Wenatchee Heights. Against the backdrop of a politically divided landscape in our nation and threat of an ever-expanding war in the Middle East, there is something about that brilliant crossbeam that speaks of hope. The cross lifts our gaze and invites us to look beyond the headlines to the One who choreographs human history.

Have you ever thought of the cross as being a "plus sign?" That concept occurred to me several years ago in preparation for a sermon.

For Christians, the cross is more than just the first century equivalent of an electric chair. It is a symbol of God's redeeming grace. In the cross we glimpse light in the darkness. We see the source of deliverance when we are helpless to save ourselves. In a world that is defined by a series of minus signs (i.e. racism, war, mass shootings, addictions, homelessness, suicide, etc.), the Creator has intersected our planet with sacrificial love and transformed a minus sign of death and despair into a plus sign of life and hope.

As I drove to Wenatchee recently to speak at an area church, I noticed the illuminated cross near the lights of Mission Ridge. It was a powerful image. It called to mind the presence of a God whose view of our lives is not obstructed by the imperfections who blind us from truly seeing each other. I wondered who was behind the gigantic cross in the distance.

I asked my brother, Marc. He told me it was a friend of his. Randy Smith. And so I reached out to Randy to discover "the rest of the story."

Back in 1994 as the Christmas season approached, longtime Wenatchee-ite Randy Smith looked over the valley and visualized a cross on a hillside overlooking the city. He couldn't get the image out of his head. "What a great symbol to call attention to what the birth of Jesus was ultimately all about," he thought. Wondering if it was a prompting from above, Randy acted on his impulse. He constructed crossbeams that were 30 feet tall. In his second version, he increased the height to 42 feet.

In 2009 an even more impressive cross of just under 110 feet tall and 50 feet wide was constructed on Wenatchee Heights. Each evening (since 2021) it is illuminated with 150 10-watt LED bulbs. The energy costs to light the cross are provided by individual contributions. And all to call attention to where our ultimate help is found.

To quote the psalmist, *"I lift up my eyes to the hills. Where will my help come from? My help comes from the Lord who made heaven and earth..."*

There is More to Life than Baseball

This is the time of year when we baseball fans find ourselves with a childlike passion for the game. The "boys of October" are family members we love to follow. Ever autumn World Series fever seems as contagious as the flu.

As our Seattle Mariners fell a game short of making the playoffs, I found myself battling boyhood blues. I was ten years old again with feelings I felt when the old Seattle Rainiers broke my heart. Once again it was painful. Losing strategic games to both the Astros and the Rangers kept us from living up to pre-season expectations. Replaying in my head all those innings we left men on base in scoring position, I had to keep reminding myself that there is more to life than baseball.

As the TV cameramen focused on the managers for the Astros (Dusty Baker) and the Rangers (Bruce Boche), I found myself reliving my daughters' childhood. Living in the Bay Area three decades ago, I introduced my three girls to my love of baseball by taking them to games in Oakland. Both Dusty and Bruce were players for the Athletics. So was future Mariners' broadcaster Bill Krueger. Being a huge baseball fan myself, I made it my goal to get Tony LaRussa, the Oakland manager, to sign caps for my kids. And I succeeded.

While watching the painful losses to both Houston and Texas, a colleague copied me in an email he'd written to a friend about one of my recent newspaper columns. John's friend's name was Craig

Reynolds. Since I was already in a nostalgic frame of mind and reliving baseball memories, I couldn't help but wonder if my friend's friend was the Craig Reynolds who had played shortstop for the Seattle Mariners in their debut season back in 1977.

I did some internet research and discovered that the Craig Reynolds my colleague knew was not a former Major Leaguer. Rather he is a local businessman running for city council in our community. My research revealed that the Craig Reynolds who was once a Seattle Mariner currently lives in Houston where he grew up.

In fact, after leaving the Mariners in 1977, "baseball player Craig" went on to play for the Astros for the majority of his career. Digging out my baseball card collection from the attic, I discovered my Craig Reynolds' card did not picture him with the Mariners but in an Astros' uniform. And, amazingly, I also found I had cards for Dusty Baker, Bruce Boche and Bill Krueger in my collection.

But I digress. I located an email address for Craig Reynolds and sent him an email asking about his life after the major leagues. To my delight, Craig replied within a couple days. His response was most gracious and informative.

Following his eleven seasons with Houston, Craig Reynolds discovered firsthand that there is more to life than baseball. Initially, he went into business with fellow Astros teammate and roommate Terry Puhl in wealth management. As an outspoken Christian, Craig incorporated the values of his faith into dealing with clients. While pursuing his career goals, Craig was pursued by a Seattle-based parachurch sports ministry to serve on their board of directors.

Pro Athletes Outreach provided a tangible network for professional athletes and their spouses to encourage balance and health in their marriages and families. In his volunteer role Craig served with other notable Seattle sports personalities including Norm Evans (former Seattle Seahawks standout) and George Toles (former public address announcer for the Seattle Supersonics) to encourage faith formation and development among their peers.

It was during this season in his life that Craig gave a message about his life and God's grace at Second Baptist Church in Houston. Following Craig's talk, Dr. Ed Young, the lead pastor at that Texas mega-church invited Craig to consider joining the church staff. That invitation given twenty-nine years ago has found Craig Reynolds ever since in the starting lineup of a pastoral team he loves.

At age seventy, the former Mariner and Astro is living his dream with his wife Josey, their three adult children and eight grandchildren. If anyone knows there is more to life than baseball, it is Craig Reynolds.

The Her Behind the Hymn

As I watched the funeral service for Supreme Court Justice Sandra Day O'Connor last year, my ears perked up as the choir at the Washington National Cathedral sang a contemporary arrangement of *Day by Day and with Each Passing Moment*. The familiar words were most timely for a grieving nation.

Help me, Lord, when toil and trouble meeting,
e'er to take, as from a father's hand,
one by one, the days, the moments fleeting,
till I reach the promised land.

The lyrics written nearly a hundred and fifty years ago are timeless. They speak of the Lord's help at those inevitable intersections on life's journey. It is a hymn that has been at the heart of my forty-five year ministry.

In fact, *Day by Day* was a hymn that my youngest daughter sang with me as a duet on Father's Day. And curiously it is a hauntingly beautiful hymn that flowed out of the broken heart of a Swedish woman who had an exceptionally close relationship with her own pastor-father.

Lina Sandell was born in Froderyd, Sweden in 1832. Because of frail health, the Lutheran pastor's daughter spent most of her childhood indoors while the neighborhood kids played outdoors. Her favorite place was in her father's study. She loved being near to the man she adored. The partial paralysis that plagued her body left her in bed much of the time. The doctors offered little hope that her condition would ever improve.

One Sunday when Lina was twelve, she had a profound experience that opened her eyes to her Heavenly Father's love. While her parents were at church, Lina was at home reading her Bible and praying. Without explanation, she found the unexpected strength to get out of bed and dress herself. When Pastor Sandell and his wife returned home, they found a healthy daughter freely walking. It was a miracle!

Lina's supernatural healing resulted in a growing sensitivity to the Lord. She began to write poetry as a means of expressing her gratitude to God. She published a volume of her work at the age of sixteen. Seven years later she wrote a hymn that celebrated the fatherlike compassion of God. *Children of the Heavenly Father* pictured a loving Father who envelops those who belong to Him in protective arms in good and bad times.

When Lina was twenty-six a tragic event would find her trusting in her *Father's wise bestowment* more than ever. She and her father were enjoying an excursion on Lake Vattern when the boat on which they were passengers suddenly lurched causing Pastor Sandell to lose his balance and fall overboard. To her horror, Lina watched her beloved daddy drown.

Amazingly, by the time Lina celebrated her twenty-eighth birthday, she had lost her father and her mother and her sister to death. Truly her trust in a loving Father was tested. For five years she navigated the slippery slope of grief all the while reflecting on God's grace against the backdrop of loss.

When she was thirty-three years of age, the words of *Day by Day and with Each Passing Moment* flowed from her fountain pen. They offered a theology of hope in the midst of suffering and pain. As was true in *Children of the Heavenly Father*, Lina compared God's faithful care to that of an earthly dad. Given her unusually close relationship to her late father, she had just cause to make such a comparison. And Lina knew only too well the intersection of toil and trouble. What she didn't know is that she would find herself at those crossroads yet again.

Two years after writing *Day by Day*, Lina married Oscar Berg, a wholesale merchant who would become a member of Sweden's Parliament. Their only child, a girl, was still born. Later Oscar would lose his business. Still, Lina found the ability to hold on to the Father's hand a day at a time.

Day by day, and with each passing moment,
strength I find to meet my trials here;
Trusting in my Father's wise bestowment,
I've no cause for worry or for fear.
He, whose heart is kind beyond all measure,
gives unto each day what He deems best,
Lovingly, its part of pain and pleasure,
mingling toil with peace and rest.

Rejection is Not Final!

When someone asks you *"What's a movie you've recently seen that you'd recommend?"* What would be your response?

My wife and I don't have to think twice about what we'd recommend. As you might recall from my column last week, *"The Boys in the Boat"* is at the top of our list. But there is another movie we recently rented *On Demand* at home. It's called *"A Million Miles Away."* We loved it so much we've watched actually watched it three times with various friends and family.

The movie is based on the inspiring true story of Jose Hernandez. Growing up in a transient Mexican farm worker's family, Jose faced obstacles of harsh labor, sleep deprivation, poverty and language. But this brilliant kid overcame the challenges of his childhood to become our nation's first migrant NASA astronaut.

If you've seen *"A Million Miles Away,"* you know that young Jose was fascinated by space from the time he was old enough to identify the Big Dipper. The movie also portrays Jose's perseverance. He applied to NASA eleven times following graduate school. And each time he was rejected. His single-mindedness was mindboggling. Although turned down repeatedly, he refused to give up. His determination to realize his dream could not be deterred.

The movie actually shows Jose saving his rejection letters. Those letters became tangible trophies that documented the painful process he'd experienced on the path to reaching his goal. Seeing Jose's stack of "thanks-but-no-thanks" responses resonated with me. I have my own stack.

Forty years ago when I began to hone my skills as a writer, I sent articles to editors in hopes of being published. More often than not, my inquiries were met with polite expressions of non-interest. For whatever reason, I decided to save my rejection letters in a manila file folder. To be honest, it was discouraging to see the file grow thicker and thicker. I was turned down by religious periodicals, travel magazines, greeting card companies and hymnal publishers. At least the variety of letterhead logos atop each negative reply made for an interesting collection.

But like Jose, I refused to give up. Gradually my three-ring binders of published articles more than compensated for the folder of letters that documented my failed attempts. Four decades later I still have that notorious file that calls to mind the pain of rejection. It serves as a reminder of the difficult process of getting published as well as what I've learned from the setbacks that are part of living.

In a letter to a group of first century Christians in Rome, the Apostle Paul calls attention to the payoff that is associated with resilience. For Paul, who was no stranger to rejection and setbacks, hardships become stepping-stones that in turn lead to a desired destination. He wrote, *"...not only so, but we also glory in our sufferings, because we know that suffering produces perseverance; perseverance, character; and character, hope."* **(Romans 5:3-4)** In other words, tough times are the means by which we exercise our faith muscles. And tears irrigate the soil of experience out of which grows a harvest of blessings.

It's true! Temporary delays make the realization of sweet dreams all the more sweet. Denied outcomes motivate revised plans or renewed efforts. A rejection letter can actually be a love letter in disguise.

Reflecting on a Somber Anniversary

On November 22, 1963 I was a sixth grader in room 19 at Liberty Elementary School in Marysville. It was my favorite grade of elementary school. That was mostly the case because Mr. Thacker was the first male teacher I'd had. Because he was a man and because he was only about 16 years older than I was, I related to him very well.

I can't recall what Mr. Thacker was teaching about that morning, but I do remember that I had a case of the hiccups. I walked to the back of the classroom to get a drink of water. It was while I was stooping to reach the water fountain attached to the sink that the voice of our principal came over the intercom. Miss Ebert informed us that President Kennedy was dead. Within the hour classes were dismissed and we were sent home.

That Friday afternoon began the longest weekend in my memory to that point. Regular television programming was interrupted by somber music. Everything appeared to be happening around me in slow motion. For an eleven-year-old, it was surreal.

Since my pastor-father was out of town on a speaking assignment, my mom took us out to a fast-food restaurant. Afterwards we stopped at a variety store. I begged her to be able to buy a JFK doll that I'd seen before. The twelve-inch figure was seated in a wooden rocking chair. When you wound the key beneath the chair (much like the key to a music box) the chair would rock back and forth playing *"Happy Days are Here Again."* In spite of my young age, I knew it would be a collectable item someday. But even more than that, it was a keepsake of someone I greatly admired. I loved President Kennedy even more than I loved Mr. Thacker (and I liked him a lot). Let me explain.

When John Kennedy was running for President in 1960, I celebrated my eighth birthday. One of the gifts I'd requested was a paperback book that I'd seen at our local grocery story. I was impressed with JFK's good looks. He was young. I was impressed by his sense of humor and his strong Bostonian accent. Since my folks were diehard Republicans, they weren't inclined to honor my wishes. But when my birthday rolled around, I was delighted to receive what I'd asked for.

After Kennedy was elected and began holding press conferences, I watched on our black and white TV set. I would often stand in front of the bathroom mirror and pretend I was the President talking to the media. I practiced talking like him. My version of *"Ask not what your country can do for you…"* sounded very much like him. When I would visit my dad at his church office after school, I stood at the pulpit impersonating my hero with an adlib speech.

So Kennedy's sudden unexpected death impacted me greatly. I was stunned. The day after he was killed, I designed a make-shift protest sign (JFK Why?) and taped it to my blue Schwinn bicycle. I pedaled up and down 3rd street expressing my anger and sorrow.

On Sunday morning I dressed for church. While my brother and I waited for our mom to get ready, we watched the television set in the family room. Since there was no regular programming, what we saw was live coverage of the suspected assassin of President Kennedy being transferred from the Dallas police station. As we watched, we saw Jack Ruby shoot Lee Harvey Oswald in front of the attending officers and reporters covering the scene. It was unreal. Later, after returning from church, we learned Oswald had died from his injuries.

Losing a childhood hero as an eleven-year-old kid opened my eyes to the fact that evil inhabits our world and that things happen all around us all the time that change the course of history. The killing of a beloved President would be the first of other assassinations of public figures within the next half dozen years. I realized life is precious and even the most powerful are not immune from tragedy. It is a life lesson that I continue to embrace as a seventy-one-year-old.

Let's Hear It for Leftovers

I love Thanksgiving! Of all the major family holidays it is the one that is relatively stress-free. There are no gifts to buy and wrap. No decorations to put up and take down. No cards to address and send. And the theme of the day is gratitude.

But perhaps the best part of Thanksgiving for me comes the day after. No, I'm not referring to Black Friday. The day after the holiday means the opportunity to eat leftovers. In our family we feast on turkey remains for the balance of the weekend. There are hot turkey sandwiches and turkey noodle soup.

But my favorite is a sandwich made of leftover turkey on bun with melted cheese, a couple strips of crisp bacon and a dollop of Roquefort dressing. It's so good! It's to die for. (At least that's what Tom the turkey said.) We call it a "turkle burkle." It's a specialty the O'Brien family served at their popular Turkey House restaurants back in the day. The Turkey House chain is no longer, but the O'Brien's famed sandwich survives in our home.

And since I brought up the subject, there is something about leftovers that is worth contemplating. I'm thinking of my parents (may their memory be blessed) who grew up in the Great Depression. As a result of surviving hard times, they had a hard time throwing away things. They saved leftover wrapping paper after giving gifts at birthdays and Christmas. They salvaged disposable cups after parties and picnics.

The laundry room cupboard held Mason jars of buttons and screws and fabric swatches. Even their clothes closets contained outfits my folks hadn't worn in twenty years. *"You never know when something might come in handy"* was their mantra.

Mom and Dad's reluctance to let go of leftover items was no doubt the result of watching their own parents creatively survive the lean years of rations and deprivations. They'd straighten bent nails to reuse, mend broken eyeglasses with string and save old car parts for spares. Leftover coffee from the percolator was reheated the next morning. Outgrown outfits were handed down as the children grew up. Bones from the chicken dinner after church were boiled to create broth. Bananas that had gone bad became the necessary ingredients for the banana bread batter. And speaking of bread, leftover stale bread became the makings of Grandma's famed pudding.

When our family spent the summer of 1987 in Nome, Alaska on a short-term mission, we discovered the mindset of living in an arctic village. You didn't throw away broken down cars, snowmobiles, appliances or toys. You leave them outside in front of your home. The cost of transporting new items by boat or plane is so expensive, you learned to utilize used parts you had saved. The value of holding on to what might be useful more than made up for the fact that many a home resembled that of Sanford and Son.

This weekend as I reflect on God's blessings in my life and that of my family, I am mindful of what God has provided for face the uncertainty of coming days. The Scriptures indicate that we are in possession of a wealth of spiritual resources to which people of faith are entitled. Like my grandparents found as they raised kids in the grueling days of the Great Depression, we have all we need to survive. We have experiences of life that have found us focused on God to look back on. They are experiences that have left us with a reservoir of memories that can be fashioned into faith and hope.

According to Saint Peter, the cupboards of our hearts contain Mason jars filled with bits and pieces that will come in handy as we seek to survive challenging days. In his second letter to first century followers of Christ, Peter writes: *His divine power has given us everything we need for a godly life through our knowledge of him who called us by his own glory and goodness.*

So how about it? Don't simply settle for watching football while eating leftovers this weekend. Allow your reheated turkey sandwich to be a trigger for considering how to creatively cobble together a life of faith by looking inside at what you have to work with.

Remember, to Say Thanks

When a friend turned fifty sometime back, I wrote this humorous rhyme:

You've reached the age where once again you play at hide and seek.
Your playmates aren't the kids next door, but facts you try to speak.
So much of what you once recalled gets stuck inside your mind.
Like popcorn hulls between your teeth, some thought get caught you find.
But gratefully it's just a stage. It's not a total loss.
You'll do just fine if you can find a string of mental floss.

But truth be told, loss of memory is no laughing matter. In my ten years as a chaplain at a retirement community, I observed the downside of aging. Growing older comes with the inevitable losses associated with the increased number of candles on our birthday cake. There is the loss of energy. There is the loss of strength and dexterity. There is the loss of hearing. Sadly, there can be the loss of a mate. And, too often, there can also be the loss of memory.

In addition to shepherding individuals in our memory care facility during the final months of their lives, I experienced the challenges of memory loss on a personal level. I watched my own mother navigate the confusing maze of Alzheimer's Disease over the course of a decade. Gratefully, my little mom never lost her ability to express love to her family or acknowledge her gratitude to God. And she never forgot how to play the piano. She was playing hymns on the baby grand in her care facility up until a couple weeks before she died.

Dementia is an unkind companion of too many people we love. The cost it exacts far exceeds what families pay out for residential care. And yet I've come to see that it's not just the elderly who exhibit memory loss. As a man of the cloth, I have witnessed in my forty-five years of ministry the frequency with which people of faith forget the faithfulness of God. I call it spiritual dementia.

Spiritual dementia is the tendency we have as humans to lose sight of times in our lives when prayers have been answered. We tend to forget how God's presence sustained us in the midst of heartache or hardship. Having learned lessons of trust through trials and challenges, it is so easy to lose sight of how God came through in the past. The Old Testament is filled with examples of the Children of Israel not remembering what they had once known. And the tendency of God's people to forget milestones of deliverance and provisions resulted in a lack of gratitude and an abundance of problems.

Remembering is the key. Long before my mom dealt with the demons of memory loss, she taught my brother and me the correlation between memory and gratitude. As little boys we heard our mom repeatedly remind us to *"remember to say thanks"* whenever we were invited to family friends for dinner. But her reminder to polite extends far beyond having good manners. *"Remember to say thanks"* is the two-step dance that enables us to recognize just how wealthy we really are. Being grateful is the by-product of looking back at our blessings. No wonder I have never forgotten my mom's refrain.

As this season of Thanksgiving approaches, I find myself focused on the importance of remembering. In our family we take time between the main meal and dessert to go around the table and verbalize those things for which we are thankful. Generalities are not permitted. Specifics are what is expected. And specifics are not all that hard to come up with if time has been spent reflecting on the goodness of God over the past year.

The author of Psalm 107 knows the correlation between memory and gratitude. Note how he begins his instructions: *"Give thanks to the* LORD, *for he is good; his love endures forever. Let the redeemed of the* LORD *tell their stories…"*

So what's your story? Looking back and reviewing the goodness of the Lord will remind you that gratitude is not a mindless exercise. It takes focus and concentration. It takes remembering. Memory is the key!

The Tragic Story Behind a Timeless Hymn

One of the most-loved hymns of all times was inspired by a tragic accident that took place one-hundred-fifty years ago this month. But to appreciate the rest of the story, you have to picture what took place two years prior.

As Horatio Spafford sat with his wife, Anna, and their four daughters at Thanksgiving in November 1871, he had to think twice when asked to pass the sugar bowl. Life had been anything but sweet in recent weeks. On October 9th, the successful Chicago attorney anxiously watched as the wind-swept flames of the Great Chicago Fire swallowed up ten square blocks of office buildings and homes along Lake Michigan. Among the smoldering ash heaps were several of Spafford's prized investment properties.

The God-fearing lawyer, who was a personal friend of evangelist Dwight L. Moody, had lost a fortune. It is also quite likely that the words of the apostle Paul stuck in Horatio's throat while he swallowed his turkey dinner: *"Give thanks in everything; for this is God's will for you..."* (1 Thess. 5:18).

How could he be grateful when life was anything but sweet? But as he looked around the family table at his beloved Anna and his four darling daughters, Spafford realized his true wealth had not gone up in smoke. He sensed the presence of a faithful God. How very grateful he was for a godly wife who was teaching their girls to love Jesus. But two short years later, Horatio sat alone at an empty Thanksgiving table. No turkey or pumpkin pie. No appetite. A grateful, yet broken heart once again pulsated with pain. And thus begins *"the rest of the story."*

In an effort to move beyond the devastation surrounding their financial ruin from the fire, the Spaffords had planned an extended family vacation in England. The family of six had traveled by train to New York to board a ship. Sadly, unexpected business dealings had required Horatio to return to Chicago just as the family was about to embark. He had waved good-bye to his wife and four girls, ages 2 to 11, as the *Ville du Havre* sailed out of New York harbor toward England. He had assured them he would join them in a few weeks.

And then the unthinkable. The vessel had collided with another ship in the North Atlantic. Within twelve minutes the *Ville du Havre* had sunk as 226 passengers lost their lives. Although many, including Horatio's wife, had been saved by the crew of another ship, all four Spafford daughters had drowned. Upon reaching England, Anna had sent her husband a telegram. As Horatio sat alone on Thanksgiving 1873, he could only ponder his wife's telegram summarized by two words: *Saved alone.*

In his grief, he was grateful his sweetheart had been spared. He gave thanks that all his girls were safe with Jesus now. He found the inner strength to celebrate that God was in control. Having sensed God's peace in the aftermath of the Great Chicago Fire two years earlier, he had learned that the granules of God's grace could sweeten the bitter taste of tragedy. Beneath the ache of his broken heart, he felt an unexplainable peace. In the depth of his soul, all was well.

Spafford booked passage for England to join Anna. When the ship sailed near the area where the *Ville du Havre* had gone down, Horatio stood on the deck looking out at the icy and angry ocean. Reaching into his coat pocket and finding a sheet of hotel stationery, he proceeded to pen a poem articulating his emotions. Little did he know his lines would be sung as a hymn in churches for ages to come:

"When peace, like a river, attendeth my way,
When sorrows like sea billows roll;
Whatever my lot, Thou has taught me to say,
It is well, it is well with my soul."

As I anticipate a gathering around the Thanksgiving table later this month, I plan to read aloud the lyrics of *"It Is Well with My Soul."* Might you consider doing the same? The words born out of heartache continue to nourish the faith of those grateful for God's blessings in a less-than perfect world.

The Innkeeper Has a Name

For those Christians who follow the liturgical church year, Christmas is not just a day but a season. It's a season that continues for a dozen days until Epiphany (January 6th). That concept is illustrated in the popular holiday song "The Twelve Days of Christmas."

As a result, our family leaves our decorations up when many Christmas trees and wreaths are deposited curbside. Our tree remains lit. Alexa continues to play the carols and our Fontanini nativity figures remain in position at the entrance to our family room.

In our nativity scene, we have the innkeeper and his family next to the holy family in the stable. And this neighboring family bears a striking resemblance to our family. There is a husband and wife and three daughters. Like me, the innkeeper figure is mostly bald. Through the years we've even added a son-in-law and grandchildren.

Truth be told, the account of Christ's nativity in the Gospel of Luke does not actually make reference to an innkeeper. But it does refer to the fact that Mary's baby was born in a barn because there was "no room in the inn." So, it's fair to infer that there likely was someone who, recognizing their plight, directed Joseph and Mary to the only available shelter on his property.

The other day as I took time to ponder these plastic figures and the story they represent, I had a new insight. The person who offered the stable to the expectant couple was actually practicing a principle that the newborn baby would one day teach as an adult rabbi. In Matthew 25 Jesus acknowledges that when we care for individuals in need (the homeless, the hungry, the sick and the imprisoned) we are showing love for Him. In essence He said, "When you serve the least of these, you are serving me."

Even before Jesus was born, the innkeeper was serving Him by serving the homeless refugee teenager who was carrying Him. He was figuratively (and literally) doing what Jesus would later call all His followers to do. And he's not the only "innkeeper" to serve God by serving others.

This Christmas season I am thinking of a modern-day innkeeper who began a life-changing organization one hundred years ago this year. His name was Abraham Vereide. He was a Methodist pastor in Seattle who came from Norway as an immigrant in the early 1900s. Touched by the plight of the poor and disadvantaged in his adopted city, Pastor Vereide sought out local business leaders to find a tangible way to influence their community for good. And so, Goodwill Industries was begun in 1923. With $475 and a dream, Pastor Vereide rallied a group of Seattle businessmen to help provide employment, education and economic opportunities for those struggling to get by.

From the start, Seattle Goodwill collected used clothing and furnishings and hired individuals to repair and sell recycled items. Their initial motto was *"Not charity but a chance."* Giving those who struggle a chance and giving used items a chance for a second life remains their mission a century later.

As an immigrant, Pastor Vereide understood the challenges of the refugee. And from the very beginning of this humanitarian organization, Seattle Goodwill has attempted to bridge the gap created by unemployment, discrimination and racial prejudice. Like the Bethlehem innkeeper, Vereide made sure those who worked with him looked out for others for Christ's sake.

The rest of Pastor Vereide's life was punctuated by a similar concern for others. During the economic downturn of the 1930s, he regularly met with Seattle's mayor Arthur Langley and other city leaders. When Langley was elected Governor, he asked Pator Vereide to convene the first ever Governor's Prayer Breakfast.

Eventually word of what was happening in the Evergreen State reached the White House. President Eisenhower called on the founder of Seattle Goodwill to created goodwill among lawmakers in Washington D.C. And, thus, the Presidential Prayer Breakfast Movement was born.

Seventy years later this amazing phenomenon, that finds lawmakers from across the aisle meeting for Bible study and prayer, continues. And, oh by the way, I know about Pastor Vereide because he was the minister who performed my Norwegian grandparents' wedding in 1921.

Looking for Aslan in Everyday Life

Long before "The Lion King" was released as an animated movie or a Broadway musical, another lion reigned in the hearts of children in the English-speaking world. His name was Aslan, a Christ-like figure who ruled an imaginary kingdom in the Chronicles of Narnia.

Seventy-one years ago, a British novelist by the name of C.S. Lewis first introduced the world to a lion that was good but not always safe. On October 16, 1950 Lewis published "The Lion, the Witch and the Wardrobe" in which Aslan was the ever-present guardian and provider. It was the first of eight books in which the kingly lion pointed the reader to a benevolent Creator.

My introduction to Aslan was in the form of a play performed by a drama troupe from Seattle Pacific University in the fall of 1974. I had just graduated from this outstanding Christian liberal arts institution and accepted a position in the university relations office. My job found me arranging tours for various performing groups on campus. When the Chancel Players were presented the opportunity to perform *"The Lion, the Witch and the Wardrobe"* by C. S. Lewis at Expo '74 in Spokane, I traveled with them.

Never having read any of The Chronicles of Narnia in my youth, I was intrigued by the character known as Aslan as presented in the Lewis' story.

Thirty-five years later I found myself depositing two of my daughters on the campus of Wheaton College in suburban Chicago. Having helped them unload their belongings, I went about exploring the campus.

I was delighted to discover the Wade Center named for the founder of ServiceMaster Company. Within this attractive brick building is contained archived materials and memorabilia related to C.S. Lewis, J.R.R. Tolkien, Dorothy Sayers and G. K. Chesterton. The writing desks of Tolkien and Lewis are displayed along with the wardrobe from Lewis' childhood home after which his most famous of all the Narnia chronicles is named. I was thrilled by what I saw.

I looked beyond Lewis' wardrobe to see a beautiful framed painting of Aslan hanging on a wall. It reminded me of the lion sculpture that graces my desk in my office. By now I had come to an informed understanding of Lewis' symbol. The lion is a powerful reminder of an ever-present God who was committed to my wellbeing. I loved the fact that Aslan was capable of making appearances without fanfare. It seemed as though he was always present even when not visible. He was a means of salvation when all seemed lost.

A dozen years after that self-guided tour of the Wade Center on the campus of Wheaton College, COVID threatened our world. During this time of lockdown and restrictions as well as fear and anxiety, I noted a number of coincidences that focused my perspective in a heavenly direction. These happenstances reminded me that in spite of being socially distanced, I was not on my own.

My friend SQuire Rushnell refers to such serendipities as Godwinks. In fact, SQuire is the one who coined the term. And during the difficult months of COVID, God, like Aslan, made His presence known at just the right time in unanticipated ways. I began observing Godwinks all around me. I started to sense the hot breath of an uncaged lion on my neck. I knew Aslan was near.

During lockdown, I resorted to my favorite pastime. Sitting at my laptop, I painted word pictures while dusting for divine fingerprints. The result is a collection of poetry in which I celebrate the presence of God in our everyday lives. I've called this volume *"When God Speaks:*

Listening for Aslan in Everyday Life." It's an interactive workbook in which each poem is paired with a prompt or question and the space for the reader to reflect and respond.

Copies of *"When God Speaks"* can be ordered from Lulu.com

A Tribute to a Maestro

As the world focuses its attention on Israel with prayers for peace, I am grieving the death of a Jewish friend who died in Tel Aviv a month and a day before the Hamas invasion.

Abraham Kaplan was an immigrant from Israel who left our world a better place. This amazing musical genius was born in 1931 seventeen years before his homeland became an independent nation. Like his gifted father before him, Abe was a celebrated choral conductor.

I first met the maestro about fifteen years ago. Abe was sitting outside the drive-thru Starbucks on Mercer Island with a conductor's score spread out on a table in front of him. I introduced myself and inquired what he was doing. Continuing to grasp his number 2 pencil, he looked up at me with a smile and described his process of scoring an original composition.

As one who has sung in choral groups since high school, I sought out more information. My interest was of obvious interest to this older gentleman with flowing white hair. We chatted for more than a few minutes. He told me of his career at Julliard and how he worked alongside Leonard Bernstein. He described his love of teaching at the University of Washington before entering retirement. But Abe hastened to add how he continued to make time to create music even after Social Security had kicked in. He shared how he felt at home at this Starbucks doing his work.

I felt like I had found a kindred spirit. In addition to sharing Abe's love of coffee, I, too, claimed this sacred space as my remote office. I often met parishioners or conducted church business at "St. Arbucks," As a result I repeatedly ran into Abe composing or arranging. Our friendship developed. We never lacked for topics to talk about.

When my musician friend Mark Thallander, the former organist at the Crystal Cathedral, was in Seattle for a series of performances, I gave him a tour of our community. Stopping at Starbucks for a caffeine boost, I saw Abe in his favorite chair by the fireplace. I proceeded to introduce Mark to him. As the two talked, I discovered that had mutual friends and shared a common memory. Mark was the organist at the dedication services at Robert Schuller's glass church three decades earlier when the Cathedral Choir sang music Abe had written for the occasion.

What? My Jewish friend had composed music for a Christian congregation? It wasn't long before I asked Abe if he would conduct the sanctuary choir at the local Covenant church where I served as pastor. He declined. He was used to a much larger venue than our little church. Our amateur group of singers lacked the skill compared with those with whom he was used to working. I refused to give up. When I saw him next, I once again pleaded my case. He hesitated. He wasn't sure we could afford what he customarily received as an honorarium.

I decided not to push it. He was right. His professionalism and experience were deserving of more than we could afford. I would just be content with a growing friendship cemented by grande lattes.

I invited Abe to have dinner with Wendy and me in our home. He willingly accepted the invitation and brought along an autographed copy of his memoirs. Over my wife's amazing manicotti, Abe regaled us with stories of famous people he had met and worked with. It was a memorable evening. And the payoff was a sudden (and unexpected) change of heart. He told me he would be willing to be guest conductor of our little church choir some Sunday.

That turned out to be a Sunday I will never forget. The choir, along with Jim Jansen our pianist and my daughter Lauren on flute, brought to life Abe's original composition "The Lord is My Shepherd." There, at the front of our sanctuary, a Reformed Jew led a group of Evangelical Christians. Abe beamed with joy as the musicians followed his lead.

I, too, was beaming. An investment in friendship between individuals of different faith traditions had resulted in a very special moment. It was a picture I will forever cherish of the harmony that is possible when we allow our lives to be instruments of God's peace.

The Tale of the Returned Letter

My recent retirement has found me sorting, tossing, saving and giving away personal effects that have helped define forty-five years of ministry. While purging manila folders of correspondence I've held on to, I came across an envelope I mailed thirty-three years ago that was returned unopened.

To be honest, I had totally forgotten about my attempt to communicate with Dave Dravecky, a former pitcher for the San Francisco Giants. And because I had no memory of what the letter was about, I decided to open the envelope to see what I had attempted to send him. To my amazement I found the letter contained the introduction to my 1990 Easter Sunday sermon:

This is the season when we remember a man from humble beginnings. He achieved remarkable popularity while barely thirty years of age. The curious and the faithful followed him wherever he plied his trade. With regularity he stood on a hill surrounded by approving crowds and with eloquence delivered his pitch. A pitch which called for response.

Some watched. Some waited. Some just kept walking. Some stood up to him and hit him in an attempt to get rid of him prematurely. Some returned from whence they had come dejected by the demands he threw their way. But regardless of the varied responses, they all respected him. His words were different. His life was refreshing. He amazed the masses with great wonders that appeared to be sleight of hand. But in all he said and did, it was obvious he knew what he believed and challenged both the young and old to follow.

And then it happened. The unthinkable. At just thirty-three years of age, his career was cut short. At the zenith of his success, his "life" was over. His faithful followers were shocked by the tragic turn of events. They grieved his loss. Their friend was gone. Finished… but not forgotten.

Again, the unexpected. Barely buried by his critics who said he'd never rise again, he reappeared with power in his hand. His band of friends were elated. The crowds were astounded. It was the comeback of all times…

My congregation in the San Francisco Bay Area assumed I was referring to the resurrection of the thirty-three-year-old rabbi from Nazareth. And for good reason. That was my intent. But then with Paul (*The Rest of the Story*) Harvey surprise, I then told them my comments were in reference to Dave Dravecky. In his own "resurrection" story, this much-loved pitcher everyone knew had recently made an unexpected comeback after being diagnosed with a cancerous desmoid tumor on his pitching arm. Surprising everyone, he'd returned to his team and succeeded. Much like the Savior he followed, Dravecky was a powerful example of faith and resilience.

Then just months prior to my Easter message, Dravecky's return to the pitcher's mound was marred by a broken bone, the return of the cancer and the amputation of his pitching arm. And through it all, this man of faith voiced his confidence in God. His career was ended, but not his influence.

Looking back thirty-three years, it all came back to me. I had wanted to share my Easter comments with an athlete I'd never met as a way of expressing my gratitude for his example. And that's why I attempted to write to Dave Dravecky. But he never received my mail. He never knew how grateful I was for his personal testimony.

But Dravecky is not the only one who refuses to give up. I discovered that the one-time Bay-Area celebrity now works in the front office of the San Francisco Giants organization. Researching a mailing address, I just this week forwarded my letter on. Whether he responds or not, I have the satisfaction of knowing that he will likely read what I wrote and understand what I felt at the time.

And speaking of letters. The New Testament is comprised of quite a few letters that have survived more than two thousand years. They are correspondence written on behalf of a Holy God who has communicated His compassion and concern for those He created in His image. And as with my letter to Dave Dravecky, it is not too late to read what has been written.

A Different Kind of Rock Collection

Have you ever stopped to think how many references there are to rocks in the Wenatchee Valley? It's amazing. As I drive over Blewett Pass from the Seattle area to visit family, I can't help but notice The Rock convenience store just prior to the intersection State Highway 970 and U.S. Highway 2. And that's just for starters.

I grew up at the base of Saddle Rock mountain. My brother lives just off Western Street in the shadow of Castlerock mountain. There is Rock Island Dam just south of East Wenatchee. There is Rocky Reach Dam just north of town. And just beyond Rock Reach, there is Lincoln Rock at Swakane Canyon. I went to high school with Rocky Skalisky and my youth pastor at Wenatchee First Assembly of God was a guy by the name of Bob Stone.

I guess you might call that a kind of rock collection. During this month of October, I've focused on another group of rocks I've gathered over the past few years. They are hand-painted works of art found in a forest near to where my wife and I live. I've featured these individual stones in a daily podcast I've called ROCKTOBER.

During COVID anonymous artists in our community painted small stones and hid them like Easter eggs at the base of a tree, perched on a stump or camouflaged in a flowering bush. The purpose was to encourage walkers during the pandemic with beautiful scenes or inspiring slogans contained on these rocks. Discovering these hidden pieces of art was a source of joy for those who found them.

A few of my favorites include a fox looking up at falling leaves, a colorful scripted reminder that "you are loved," and one that simply invites me to DREAM. These unexpected finds were like finding buried treasure when our future health and hopes were masked by uncertainty.

There's another rock that I'm contemplating this month. It, too, is an unexpected find that offers hope to those attempting to navigate life in the valley of death's shadows. It's a large stone that gives me the confidence to be bolder (than I might otherwise be) when encouraging friends and family imprisoned by fear and grief. It's a stone I've never seen up-close and personally but one I have spent much of my life contemplating. And recently I saw a facsimile of the same.

While exiting Lumen Field in Seattle a couple of weeks ago following the Seahawks game, I noticed a large stone-like sculpture near the street. It was a massive boulder about five feet high and four feet wide. When I saw it, my mind raced to the stone described in the New Testament that was used to seal the tomb in which a lifeless rabbi from Nazareth was buried. It is the same giant rock that was rolled away three days later when women friends of Jesus came to pay their respects.

So, you might ask, why am I contemplating the message of Easter in October? Everyone knows that Holy Week, Good Friday and Easter are holy days associated with the spring. And yet there is no denying that the message of the empty tomb has year-round implications. If death has been defeated once and for-all (literally), then it is good news that continues to rock our world on a daily basis. Early Christians moved their weekly day of worship from Saturday (the Jewish Sabbath) to Sunday (the day when Jesus' grave was discovered to be empty). The resurrection of Jesus was considered the hinge pin on which the truth of the entire Gospel rested (see Saint Paul's words in 1 Corinthians 15:14). Is it any wonder ancient believers who gathered on Sundays referred to the Lord's Day as "little Easter?"

With that in mind, I'm inclined to refer to the massive rock that was rolled away from Jesus' grave as "stone hinge." And as I ponder the various rocks that are part of my collection, this "stone hinge" is the most valuable to be sure.

What I Learned from Playing Barbies

When the Barbie movie was released, I suggested to my wife that we go. And to those who know me, it should come as no surprise that I suggested we go wearing pink. Yes, I have a couple pink shirts in my closet. Sadly, the film had left the theaters before our schedules would allow us to see Ryan Gosling and Margot Robbie on the big screen. Wendy and I donned our pink attire as we watched the blockbuster hit On-Demand on our tv in the family room.

Come to think of it, watching from our family room was the perfect venue to view a fun film that triggered many memories. From the time I was a young dad I played Barbies with my three daughters in our family room. Unlike many of my fellow fathers, I had no problem sitting cross-legged on the floor giving voices to the miniature Mattel misses. I was secure enough in my masculinity to let my hair down while brushing Barbie's with my girls. In fact, it was in that unique context that I learned a few lessons that have served me well as a pastor. Consider the following:

Trust is more easily earned while meeting another on their level. My daughters LOVED the fact that I was willing to play Barbies with them. It became OUR THING. Stooping to where they were won their hearts. When I was a rookie minister, I observed an older colleague greeting his flock at the door of the church following the service. Rather than patting a child on the head, this pastor took a knee and greeted the little lamb while looking them in the eye. What I saw deeply impressed me. I made it a habit to do the same. But I also discovered the concept of finding common ground holds true with adults as well. When we seek to find common ground with another person, we are more likely to engage them without pretense.

Using one's imagination cultivates a sense of wonder. Pretending with my girls and creating conversations between the dolls stretched my ability to think outside the box. It gave me a platform for sharing life lessons with my offspring using foot-long plastic figures as a vehicle. It's amazing how much you can communicate when you are indirectly speaking.

As I look at the New Testament, I see that Jesus did the same. By sharing parables, he invited his listeners to use their imaginations. Through the use of fiction, Jesus fleshed-out truth. And I have found much freedom illustrating bottom-line convictions by sharing hypothetical anecdotes off-the-top of my head.

We are never too old to play. When I first started to dress Ken and Barbie dolls, I was in my early thirties. Now that I am seventy-one, I still find myself on the floor in the family room with my two granddaughters. Just the other day while browsing at the local thrift store, I found a toy sports car with a couple dolls strapped in the front seat. Of course, I bought it for Immy and Ivy. I can imagine hours of play with my pintsize playmates. After all, I have experience making believe.

But the family room floor isn't the only place we have fun together. There's the backyard where we play hide-and-seek. There's the street in front of our house where we roll tennis balls down a hill. And there's the park next to the thrift store where we use our imaginations and energy. And when it comes to the latter, they have three-times as much as I do.

But even so, play rejuvenates us. It provides a needed distraction from daily routines that serves to reboot our "personal" computers. Play is God's way to remind us that when all is said and done, we are His children no matter how many candles will adorn our birthday cake this year.

Let's Hear it for Mentors!

It happened fifty years ago! I had just begun my senior year of university. I was old enough to order a glass of wine, but at twenty-one I wasn't mature enough to comprehend how my career would come together.

Enter a thirty-three-year-old Presbyterian pastor by the name of John Huffman. John was the visiting cleric on campus for spiritual emphasis week at Seattle Pacific University. In addition to being the pastor of the church where Richard Nixon, our current President, often attended, this James Garner look-alike was a skilled orator. He had a way of connecting faith and life that resonated with me.

The fact that I was a Biblical literature major was an indication of my interest in a faith-focused vocation. But I was unsure of what awaited me after graduation. Somehow, I sensed that this articulate preacher might be able to help me process my uncertainty.

I booked a one-on-one appointment with John and shared with him my faith journey as well as my aspirations and options. He listened to my hopes and dreams and didn't dismiss my doubts. I felt understood by someone who understood where I was and where I was likely headed. I had no idea as I opened my heart to this virtual stranger that John Huffman would become a lifelong mentor.

Just last month John and I had lunch near his home in Southern California and celebrated a half-century of friendship. It was a meaningful meal punctuated by laughter, sighs and knowing glances. There were no limits to the amount of withdraws we could make from our memory banks. The wrinkles in our faces were evidence of the years we'd made deposits.

Looking back on the past five decades, I can identify the adhesive that glued our friendship on a strong foundation. Letters, emails, phone calls and occasional golf games nourished our long-distance relationship. Through the joyful times of courtship and marriage and the birth of my three daughters, John celebrated with me. Through the challenges of difficult pastoral transitions, John heard my hurting heart and offered wise counsel. When new opportunities to invest my experience came my way, my friend was willing to pray with me for direction.

John's role as spiritual counselor to our former president proved advantageous years later. It helped pave the way for a growing friendship with Richard Nixon's younger brother who lived in the Seattle area. When Ed Nixon passed away, I had the unique privilege of eventually officiating at his memorial service. And it is John whom I credit with my getting to know Rich Stearns, the recently retired CEO of World Vision. For years John had been the chairman of the WV Board of Trustees and developed a close working relationship with Rich.

As a result of what I have personally experienced in my relationship with John, I am a huge proponent of mentors. The power of being a modeling influence in a person's life cannot be underestimated. Mentors make a difference. Mentors lead by example. Their example inspires leadership. Mentors provide a three-dimensional picture of what is possible in any field of endeavor.

No wonder the New Testament is replete with examples of mentoring. Jesus chose twelve individuals to dog his footsteps as he barked out critical comments to the religious leadership who didn't practice what they preached. What the dozen disciples observed resulted in a perspective of what living faith looked like. And then of the twelve, the rabbi from Nazareth chose three who qualified for executive management training. In Peter, James and John. Jesus saw potential that was worthy of his personalized focus.

We can't forget Barnabas who mentored his cousin John Mark or Priscilla and Aquila who mentored Apollos. And then, of course, there was Paul who invested in the likes of Silas and Timothy. The end result is attested in the growth of the first century Church.

Mentoring equates to the multiplication of talent and the maximization of opportunities in the church and in the corporate sector. Like coaching in the NFL, mentoring provides hands-on encouragement and correctives. Mentoring is the key that unlocks future success. John Huffman was my Pete Carroll. And I can only hope that my attempts at mentoring those who looked to me for an example were as productive.

Two Men, Six Degrees and a B-52

You most likely have heard the expression "six degrees of separation." Well, you don't have to be Kevin Bacon to appreciate the truth of what that means. I recently experienced those six degrees first-hand.

My wife and I visited Port Townsend a couple weeks back for a three-day getaway with close friends. Following coffee and scones on the waterfront, we walked the main street. Having read Daniel Brown's book "The Boys in the Boat," I was fascinated with the Pocock boat house and the vintage rowing shells adjacent to the wooden boat museum. And the vintage architecture of the buildings downtown were a feast for the eyes.

When I happened into a quaint antique store, I saw a basket filled with what appeared to be old handwritten letters. As one who has a prized stamp collection, I couldn't resist exploring the contents. What I discovered were scores of hand-addressed envelopes with canceled stamps. The letters had been removed to protect the family's privacy.

Sorting through the pile, I saw many envelopes addressed to a family on Mercer Island. Since that is where I live, my interest increased. The postmark of the first envelope I investigated indicated the letter was sent from Burlington, Vermont on April 5, 1948 to a Mrs. H. W. Withington on Mercer Island. The last name seemed vaguely familiar. The address simply read Avalon Park. That was a neighborhood near to the retirement community where I've been the chaplain for the past decade. Since there was no street address, I assumed the home belonged to a prominent family.

I did some quick investigative research on my iPhone. Google gave me what I was looking for. Holden Withington and his wife Betsy were indeed prominent Mercer Island residents. They moved to the island in 1941 (just a year after the floating bridge was completed). Holden, an MIT grad, had been recruited by Boeing as an engineer. He would rapidly climb the ranks of the airplane company eventually retiring as vice-president of engineering.

But Holden's most notable claim to fame took place in 1948 when the envelope that first caught my eye was addressed. Seventy-five years ago, Holden (who went by Bob) holed-up in a hotel room with five others to design the swept-wing B-52 aircraft. An airplane that would serve the United States military operations for half a century and would serve as the prototype for the Boeing 707.

As I continued my research about the Withington family, I discovered that Bob and Betsy would eventually move into Covenant Shores. What? That's where I would work for ten years. Even though they both died before I began as chaplain, that is why their name sounded familiar to me. When Bob passed, he was the last surviving member of the team of six who had designed the B-52. His wife would die two weeks before I started working at the Shores.

I also discovered that the Withingtons' neighbor at Covenant Shores was General Guy Townsend. What? This brigadier general, test pilot and combat veteran had been a friend of mine and fellow Rotarian before he died. And I had the privilege of being chaplain to Guy's widow Anne until my retirement this summer.

As my iPhone investigation into the past concluded, I came to see that both the Withingtons and the Townsends were more than just neighbors. Their lives were bookends of sorts. Whereas Bob had helped design the B-52, Guy had been at the controls of the very first

B-52 when it took off on its test flight from Boeing field enroute for Larson Air Force Base in Moses Lake on April 15, 1952 (three days before I was born). And get this. Both men died in 2011.

Who would have guessed that glancing into that basket of envelopes at that Port Townsend antique shop would find me connecting so many dots? Certainly not me. But it got me reflecting on how small our world really is. And as the Frank Capra movie "It's a Wonderful Life" celebrates, each human life impacts another in significant (in not always apparent) ways. It pays to be aware!

No Ordinary Anniversary

Most of us can recall what we were doing on September 11, 2001. I was driving to work in suburban Chicago listening to the classical music station when the announcer interrupted programming with breaking news. Upon arriving at my office, I was glued to the television dumbfounded by the tragic events I watched play out.

That Tuesday morning twenty-two years ago our nation was blindsided by terrorist attacks that would rob upwards of three thousand Americans of their lives. It was a day that would alter the way we do life and view our vulnerability. It's no wonder that it was a day is engraved on the tissues of our memory.

With each passing anniversary of that grim day, however, there is a tendency to forget the impact and the importance of what Ground Zero signified. As a result, we tend to observe September 11th without much fanfare. Familiarity breeds apathy. For example, do you recall what you were doing September 11th two years ago?

I have good reason to recall what I was doing. It was my privilege to serve as chauffer for the parents of 9/11 hero Todd Beamer as they toured our state. Perhaps you remember how that thirty-two-year-old Oracle salesman courageously led a group of passengers on Flight 93 to storm the terrorist-held cockpit announcing "Let's roll!" It was Todd's initiative along with a few others that kept that hijacked United

Airlines plane from being flown into the White House or U.S. Capitol Building (although it cost them their lives).

After hearing of Todd's story in the aftermath of 9/11, I was inspired to learn more about this young husband and father of two. Todd was a graduate of Wheaton College just a few miles from where I worked and our family was living at the time. Because I was writing a weekly newspaper column in Chicagoland, I located Todd's parents in Maryland and emailed them. I asked permission to do an interview with them about their son. They graciously consented.

Over the next couple years, I communicated regularly with the elder Beamers. Several articles in newspapers and magazines resulted that celebrated Todd's faith, family and patriotism. But I never met David and Peggy in person. Our communication was strictly through email.

Fast-forward to 2021. As the twentieth anniversary of September 11th approached, I wondered if Todd Beamer's parents would consider coming out for the ceremony held annually at the 9/11 Memorial in Cashmere. I mentioned my idea to my friend Tom Green who gave leadership to the local memorial commission. To my delight, Tom reached out to David and Peggy. I knew it would be a longshot since the Beamers would likely be in demand at much larger venues. To my surprise, the Beamers accepted the invitation.

Because I live in the Seattle area, I offered to pick the Beamers up at SeaTac. I also arranged for a couple of other speaking opportunities including the retirement community where I was chaplain and the high school named for Todd in Federal Way.

As we drove over the Cascade Mountains and dropped down into the Wenatchee Valley, my guests were thrilled by what they saw. As they met the 9/11 Memorial commission, they were equally impressed. As David responded to a FOX News interview prior to the ceremony, he acknowledged the values and patriotism of the Wenatchee Valley that bespeak the heart of America. I looked on with pride hearing how my hometown was being commended on national television.

And then came the ceremony. I'm guessing many of you were there. Following the invocation that I was invited to offer, David Beamer stood at the podium and proudly reflected on the life and death of his only son. Near the end of his message, he challenged his audience to not grow apathetic in the cause for which his son and others gave their lives. As I recall David Beamer said something to the effect of…

"Twenty years later we are still free and safe because of those who serve and sacrifice to make it so. Let us remember that enemies without and enemies within remain a threat to that freedom and security."

And now two years later, his words continue to reverberate in my mind. Every September 11th is a day for all of us to recommit ourselves to remain vigilant even as we salute our flag and pledge our allegiance to the country for which it stands.

In Praise of a Family Tree

The recent wildfires in Maui have resulted in an incalculable loss of lives and homes. The unimaginable devastation will take months to sort out. The pain and suffering will never be fully totaled. And yet that massive banyan tree in Lahaina continues to stand as a symbol of life and hope.

Against the backdrop of leveled legendary buildings and beloved landscapes now destroyed, the charred banyan tree portrays the indomitable spirit of the islands. It rises above what is lost. With branches that reach out, it pictures enveloping protection. Like the description Saint Paul uses to call attention to his own maelstrom of suffering, the tree is bruised but not broken. It is knocked down but not destroyed.

Because I have never vacationed on Maui, I have never seen that iconic tree up close and in person. I have many friends who have visited this popular Hawaiian island many times and have posted selfies with that the Lahaina tree on Facebook. It's dimensions are impressive. It reminds me of a similar tree on the island of Oahu. I have visited and photographed the banyan tree at the historic Moana Hotel on Waikiki Beach on numerous occasions.

The banyan trees in Maui and Oahu are a beautiful example of what I love about the islands. There is just something about the culture of the Hawaiian people that calls to me. The soothing music of the ukulele and the gentle movements of the hula undermine the frenetic stress that frequently imprisons us. I love the Hawaiian word *aloha*. Aloha (like the Hebrew word *shalom*) can have multiple meanings. It is most commonly used to express personal greetings such as hello and goodbye. But aloha can also be a synonym for love, peace, health or wholeness. The aloha spirit is one that suggests joy and happiness as well as belonging.

The aloha spirit is also seen in the way family is defined in our fiftieth state. The Hawaiian word for family is 'ohana. It includes more than just those who are related by sharing the same bloodline. Family is inclusive of those members of the community who are respected and loved. In Hawaii, senior citizens are referred to as uncles and aunties. Cousins are more than just those whose parents are siblings to your parents. Cousins are those loved ones who are part of your network of relationships. As a result in the islands, a family tree is not simply what Ancestry.com or 23andMe might suggest. The family tree is an ever-expanding organism of people who love each other.

With that in mind, the sight of that banyan tree on Maui calls to mind the family tree of those who are caring for each other. Those who are searching for the missing. Those who are responding to the needs of the homeless. Those who are beginning the lengthy process of rebuilding infrastructures and communities. It's a family that comforts, encourages and continues to hope. As the destructive flames and suffocating smoke have given way to swaying palms and warm tropical breezes, the family tree of Maui still stands strong and tall. It is a family tree whose roots go down deep into the soil of commitment and unconditional love.

That picture of family is how the New Testament describes the Church. The family of God is not defined by those who share the same DNA. It is a community of those who share a common allegiance to a person who modeled love for one's neighbor as well as for the marginalized and those easily forgotten. The Church is a family made up of those who view the Creator as their Heavenly Father and thus view themselves as brothers and sisters. It is a community that cares for each other with unconditional love.

For the past ten years while serving as a chaplain in a continuing care retirement community, I simplified my summer wardrobe. I only wore Hawaiian shirts every day between Memorial Day and Labor Day. It was my way of symbolizing the kind of family-like love I'm called to embody as a man of the (flowery) cloth. It was my way of saying (without words) I bring you God's aloha!

It's a Wonderful Place

Anyone who knows me knows how much I love the classic Frank Capra film "It's a Wonderful Life." There is just something about that fictional town of Bedford Falls that calls to mind a simpler time in our lives. Gower's Drugstore and the Bailey Brothers Building and Loan are emblematic of small town America where people knew each other and cared for one another.

Bedford Falls also had a movie house. In the Christmas classic that introduced the world to George Bailey and Mr. Potter, do you recall what The Bijou Theatre was showing? "The Bells of St. Mary's." (Now there's a piece of trivia to store away for a future appearance on Jeopardy.)

I'm guessing that The Bijou was a gathering place for townsfolks. Double features on Saturday afternoons found the kids munching popcorn and following the adventures of their favorite silver screen heroes. Moms and Dads kept abreast of current events by watching newsreels narrated by the unmistakable voice of Ed Hurlihy. (Would you believe Ed Hurlihy's son was a member of the church I served in Chicagoland?)

Much like the old drugstore soda fountain which defined a counter-culture long gone, time was when the local movie theatre was a fixture of our past. It provided neighbors a place to experience life together, sit side-by-side in a relaxed environment and invest in making memories. Soda fountains and movie houses were small enough so that you were known by your first name and greeted when you arrived. Oh, how I miss those days.

A couple weeks ago my wife and I had participated in an event we will long remember. We joined with locals in Chelan to celebrate the 109th anniversary of the historic Ruby Theatre. The theatre owners (Larry Hibbard and Mary Murphy, husband and wife) treated us to a wonderful evening of history, refreshments (medium combo of hot buttered popcorn and a Pepsi for $5) and an opportunity to see the very first motion picture ever screened at The Ruby back in 1914. It was a silent animated short called "Gertie the Dinosauer."

Before the memorable evening was over, we also watched Charlie Chaplin in "The Little Tramp," Buster Keaton in "The Goat" as well as Walt Disney's first animated feature "Puss and Boots." What made the experience exceptional was the fact that each of the silent films was accompanied by live music on The Ruby's "autoplay" organ.

This unusual relic was manufactured in 1919 is one of only a handful instruments of its kind still in use. She even has a name. Valentina is referred to as Ruby's younger sister. Larry Hibbard sat at the console changing player-piano rolls and manually operating the sound effects all the while matching the action on the screen. Truly amazing!

Here are a couple of other amazing facts: The Ruby was built by a couple of local brothers (the Kingmans) just two years after the Titanic sank. It was named for the daughter of the theatre's first manager. I also was impressed to discover that this Chelan landmark has operated continuously since it opened in 1914 (with the exception of the Spanish Flu pandemic of 1918 and COVID in 2020).

Situated in the heart of downtown Chelan, The Ruby is a historical gem that calls to mind the small town vibe of which most Americans only dream about. Unlike The Bijou movie house in Bedford Falls, it really exists. In fact, I love imagining it what it must have been like to have gone to The Ruby just after World War 2 ended to see "It's a Wonderful Life" for the first time. What a treat that must have been for those who did.

Like an old relative, The Ruby has seen a lot of life lived out. She has been part of a lot of history. And just like my late great-aunt Ruby Watland, she has stories to tell if we only take the time to listen. Let's not take this wonderful landmark for granted. There will likely come a day when the movie house that began by showing silent films will herself be silent. Let's enjoy her while we can. And the same goes for aging family members from whom we can still learn a lot. Ask them questions. Make time to listen. Celebrate while you can!

An Antidote to Disenchantment with Church

Church attendance in North America is declining. Churches are closing at an unprecedented rate. Those who attended Sunday school or youth group as kids are abandoning their childhood faith (or at least disengaging in organized religion) once they reach college.

Unanswered questions about how Biblical authority and cultural trends relate contribute to a generational complacency or an out-and-out rejection of spiritual values in which our children and grandchildren were raised. Societal redefining of historical Judeo-Christian norms has contributed to the confusion over and rejection of traditional faith.

But disenchantment with church is not a new phenomenon especially when church leaders have failed to practice what they have preached. Elmer Gantry-like charlatans masquerading as sincere pastors have plagued parishes for decades. Vulnerable sheep have been victimized and shorn by less-than-trustworthy shepherds. Toxic-faith syndrome has emerged as a recognized diagnosis.

Gratefully there are those who have survived such chicanery with their faith intact. My friend and longtime mentor David McKenna is one such survivor. Eight decades ago this bright adolescent was forced to come to terms with the duplicity between what he witnessed on Sundays and what he learned was being lived out during the week.

At ninety-four, this former president of a prestigious Christian liberal arts university and president emeritus of a leading theological seminary has just released his memoir. *The Triumphs of His Grace* is a spiritual odyssey chronicling his candid struggles and resultant disenchantment with the fundamentalist congregation in which he was raised.

The cautionary tales of hypocrisy and heartache that comprise each chapter make for a page-turning autobiography with which I can relate. I, too, grew up in a fundamentalist congregation where inconsistencies and Pharisee-ism threatened to derail my call to ministry.

But I am grateful that in a book, that David began writing more than forty years ago, my friend takes great care to acknowledge God's constant unwavering overtures in his young life played out against the backdrop of less-than ideal circumstances.

This one who felt drawn by the amazing grace of the Almighty at a young age documents the details of a call to Kingdom influence that resulted in a successful career in Christian higher education.

When David asked if I would read a prepublication version of his manuscript, I willingly agreed. After all, he had been my college president half a century earlier. Upon graduation, I had worked for him as his director of church relations. When I married the young woman I had first met at Seattle Pacific, David granted his blessing. I cherished our growing friendship as I completed my graduate degree and moved on into pastoral ministry. There was a reason I kept a handwritten note of encouragement from David on my desk in every one of the four congregations I served.

As I read what David had written I was fascinated to read facts about my friends I'd never known. I was encouraged by his courageous honesty. His personal struggles with his parents' faith made for challenges and opportunities by which he could come to terms with his own convictions and reengage with a God who would not let him go.

When David later asked if I would write an endorsement to his memoir, I felt honored. Having personally lived through some of the same disenchantments he documents in his book, I could commend his offering without hesitation. Here is a new book that I believe offers new options for a troubling trend in our culture. It is my personal hope that what this senior Christian statesman has published will help a younger generation of thoughtful seekers reconsider the time-tested truths of God's grace.

A Photograph Memory with Spiritual Implications

I've always been interested in taking photos. As a nine-year-old I took a picture of the partially constructed Space Needle. Impressed with the magnificent spillway, I aimed my Kodak Brownie camera at Grand Coulee Dam. The black-and-white snapshots were nothing to write home about, but I was hooked. Capturing "life as it happens" on film became a lifelong passion. Ask my family, I'm still taking more photos than most with my iPhone.

Shortly after our family moved to the Wenatchee Valley in 1964, I discovered something worthy of my camera's lens. It was the outcropping of basalt rock in Swakane Canyon that bears a remarkable resemblance to our sixteenth President. All these years later, I still am fascinated by the natural rock formation. Most every trip we make to our lake house in Chelan, I quickly glance to the left to pay my respects to Honest Abe as we pass Rocky Reach Dam.

Recently I did some research to learn about this natural phenomenon unique to our area. What was created thousands of years ago by wind, weather and the intensity of geological activity captured the imagination of those who saw it. The indigenous peoples and Caucasian explorers in our region in the early 1800s identified the rock as resembling a human's profile.

Speaking of taking photos of our famous landmark, just nine years after Washington became a state, a guy by the name of Charles Schoff took a photo of the rock formation from the deck of a Columbia River steamboat. Schoff was the engineer of the packet vessel named the *Echo* that ran between Wenatchee and Orondo. Curiously, a deckhand on the *Echo* by the name of Ed Ferguson was reading a biography of Abraham Lincoln at the time. Ed remarked to Charles that the face in the rock resembled the profile of the late President.

Schoff and Ferguson's discovery caught on. The feature became known to crew members and passengers traveling down the Columbia River as Lincoln Rock. Four years later, the July 1902 issue of The Ladies Home Journal featured another photograph of Lincoln Rock. This one was taken by a photographer by the name of M. P. Spencer. His black-and-white headshot appeared as part of an article titled "Rocks That Have Faces on Them." From that point on, the face overlooking the Wenatchee Valley had national recognition. It would take nearly eighty years, however, before Lincoln Rock State Park would be officially recognized as a tourist attraction.

What I find fascinating is that long before Abraham Lincoln was born in 1809, his likeness as an adult would be visible to inhabitants and passersby of our area. Half a century later in 1859, our beloved leader had no idea that his face was viewable on more than just printed campaign posters. When he died six years later, he was unaware that his profile would be the subject of amateur photographers like me a century in the future.

I also find it fascinating that Lincoln Rock pictures for me the process of spiritual maturity. Just as the image of Lincoln was created through extreme natural disasters like windstorms, seismic shifts and geologic trauma, so too my faith is shaped through hardships and heartaches. The God I worship is using the difficult circumstances in my life in constructive ways so that I will increasingly look like Jesus. And we all relate to the pain that accompanies spiritual growth.

In a letter to the early Christians in Rome, Saint Paul reflects on the purpose of suffering in the lives of believers. In that well-known passage where the Apostle talks about "all things working together for good," he looks back to what God saw long before anyone else had a clue. Saint Paul asserts that those God foreknew He predestined to be conformed to the image of his Son (Romans 8:29).

In other words, God saw the finished result of our being shaped into the likeness of Jesus even before we were born. And whenever I pass Lincoln Rock on my way to Lake Chelan, I have a visual aid to remind me God is still at work in my life.

Lessons from the Resurrection Tree

For the past five years I have been a faith and values columnist for the Wenatchee World. As such I have reflected on the meaning infused within the mileposts on life's journey. I've touched on such things as births, graduations, career achievements, sports accomplishments and family struggles. A frequent theme has been the fleeting and fragile nature of the human experience.

As a chaplain at a retirement community, anticipated death is a common occurrence for me. Unexpected death, on the other hand, takes your breath away. That was the situation when Bud Palmberg, my dear friend and ministry colleague, died a few weeks ago while on a preaching mission in Bali. This much-loved resident at Covenant Shores lost his balance on the way to dinner, fell and hit his head. The resulting brain injury proved fatal. The emotional impact

Since Bud has been a fixture in my life for forty years, his sudden death hit me harder than normal. As a fellow pastor seventeen years my senior, he mentored me when I was called to my first church out of seminary. We regularly played golf on Mondays. He even provided premarital counseling prior when Wendy and I got engaged. I never could have guessed that twenty-five years later I would have the privilege of being called to lead the church on Mercer Island he served for a quarter of a century. Neither could I have anticipated I would be his chaplain the last several years of his life.

Dealing with my friend's unexpected death was made a bit easier knowing he was ready to go. Whereas a significant part of my job description is helping residents "pack their bags for Heaven," Bud's bags were tagged and waiting for pick up. A sermon he gave at church a year ago called attention to his anticipation of death and his hope of resurrection. That audio clip was played at his memorial service.

About the time Bud preached on his readiness to die, another unexpected death occurred at Covenant Shores. It was a giant willow tree that has guarded our lakefront for over a hundred years. This much-loved fixture to our campus has provided shelter for many an outdoor concert.

Last July, five days following a performance by the 75 piece Bellevue Community Band, the giant tree collapsed in the middle of the night. Although we were grateful the willow had not fallen on any unsuspecting individuals, we were deeply saddened to lose a friend. The sudden loss of what we had taken for granted was devastating. The arborists were called and came to remove the limbs we had grown to love. The emotional impact was such that we even held a memorial service for the tree.

This past Easter Sunday, as I prepared to lead our annual sunrise service on the lakeshore, I walked by the stump of the old willow tree and marveled at what I saw. In the dawn's early light was picture of resurrection. New life was growing from what had died. Unexpected death had given way to signs of hope.

The "resurrection tree" has become a source of comfort to me as I grieve those in my life who have been taken from me unexpectedly. It is a beautiful reminder that people of faith do not grieve as those who have no hope.

Obviously, we grieve. Grief is an indicator that we have loved. Grief is proof of the fact that we have shared life and made memories with someone of significance to us. But as St. Paul reminds us, an empty first century grave empties grief of its hopelessness. I guess you could call that "good grief."

A Ray of Hope

I met Ray Brook in the spring of 2005. He was a lay leader in the suburban Seattle congregation that had just called me to be their pastor. Ray was part of a team of business folks in the church with a common goal. They had generously contributed to a fund that would ease the burden on a pastor moving from the Midwest to an upper-middle class community. Ray's positive personality and fervent faith was the very thing a shepherd longs for in a flock.

As my wife and I adapted to a new ministry assignment in the cloudy Pacific Northwest, this recently retired executive with Procter and Gamble was a ray of sunshine. He invited me to be his guest at the local Rotary club and then offered to sponsor me when I indicated interest in becoming a member.

When I was offered tickets to the NFC Championship game between the Carolina Panthers and the Seattle Seahawks, I invited Ray to go with me. Not only did our home town team win, I knew I had someone on my team who was committed to me succeeding in our local ministry.

The more time I spent with Ray, the more I got to know his fascinating story. I discovered why he was a ray of inspiration to those who knew him. I learned that his son was born with cystic fibrosis. Although the boy was only expected to live a few years, Ray and his wife surrounded their son with love and nurture. Ron lived twenty-six years.

Ray was grateful for the bonus years but grieved the death of his only child. Because God was not part of Ray's life at the time, he channeled his grief by staying physically fit. Bike riding and running were his go-to diversions. Running marathons and competing in triathlons became a passion. He determined that he would spend the rest of his life seeking adventure. He would face self-imposed challenges vicariously for his son as well as for himself.

When Ray retired in 2000 after thirty-five years with Procter and Gamble, he was gratified by the countless recognitions he'd received in a stellar career that had paid big dividends relationally and monetarily. But there was something in his soul that was bankrupt.

With time to do what he wanted, Ray began checking off adventures on his bucket list. He hiked the world-renown Pacific Crest Trail from Mexico to Canada over a period of five months by himself.

A few months later as Ray prepared to celebrate his sixtieth birthday, he decided to tackle an even more ambitious goal. Because his son had not lived long enough to reach his goal of riding his motorcycle from coast to coast, Ray decided he would realize Ron's dream as well as his own. He would ride his bike through all fifty states and all ten Canadian provinces.

What began in Hawaii in January 2001 concluded on the steps of the U. S. Capitol in Washington D.C. on September 9th. His amazing 17,171 mile road trip also included stopping at sixty Rotary clubs in the U.S. and Canada along the way. Ray was scheduled to be interviewed about his "60 Cycle" Adventure on The Today Show on September 12, 2001. But events of September 11th derailed those plans.

All the same Ray's personal Ground Zero would not take place for another few months. Accepting an invitation to attend an Alpha

Course (at the church where I would meet him four years later), Ray went public with his decision to follow Christ at a weekend retreat. Five weeks later his wife of forty years accidentally drowned.

Ray's relationship with Jesus and his new found family of faith helped carry him through some very difficult days. Ray felt God call him to a new adventure – a solo kayak journey the 1,000 miles of the Sea of Cortez. Amazingly it turned out to be exactly forty days and nights.

A year later the Lord would bring a woman into Ray's life that was as beautiful on the inside as she was on the outside. Gay's radiant faith brightened every room she entered. When I came to the Mercer Island Covenant Church as the lead pastor, Ray and Gay had been married for a little over a year. Not only was their love for one another unmistakable, so was the distance Ray had traveled in his walk with Christ. His spiritual wisdom and encouragement was a blessing to our congregation and me.

In 2011, as I was leaving the church to pursue other opportunities in the area, Ray was in a place of transition as well. This ray of sunshine and inspiration (and his wife) felt called to sell their home and belongings to follow the Lord's lead.

As with Abraham, they didn't know how God's plans would unfold. Initially, it meant accepting an invitation in India to teach life skills to young women who might not otherwise have the tools with which to succeed. The opportunity in India gave way to opportunities in China and then in South Africa.

Each year Ray and Gay would return to the Seattle area for medical appointments and to report back to their church and our Rotary club. Each time it was inspiring to hear how the Lord was using them.

In the spring of 2019 Ray had an operation to repair a hernia. The routine procedure revealed a more serious situation. Ray's doctor blindsided him with a diagnosis of esophageal cancer. That was the very cancer that claimed his mother's life a decade earlier.

Ray began radiation and chemo treatments. As those who had witnessed their friend's faith grow prayed, the cancer diminished in size. But then cancer in the pancreas was identified. More treatments. More prayer.

Ray lost his hair, but not his hope. This 5' 10" Yul Brenner remains a giant of faith. He continues to walk sixty miles a week while maintaining a strict exercise regimen and healthy diet.

I recently sat with Ray on the deck of the home he and Gay are renting. We reviewed the chapters in his most amazing life story. As the afternoon sun bathed us in warmth, there was a glow on Ray's smiling face. Here was a brother-in-Christ that is convinced the days of his life are in the hands of a loving Heavenly Father. Ray has faced adversity before. He knows the heartache that hardships bring. But he also is convinced that trials are opportunities to persevere and trust.

For Ray Brook, every day is a day to run with endurance the race marked out for him as he continues to look to Jesus, the author and finisher of his faith. In this world of uncertainty, I am grateful this ray of hope is brightening his sphere of influence.

Life is Like a Waiting Room

While waiting for a routine blood draw a few weeks ago, I was reminded of how often hospital waiting rooms have factored into my seventy-one years of life. Four decades ago, I received a phone call from a waiting room in another state informing me that the woman I had started dating was on life-support due to an unexpected allergic reaction.

After activating the prayer chain in the church I was pastoring, my office (just off the sanctuary) became a waiting room. Gratefully, those days of anxious waiting gave way to news that Wendy (the woman I would marry eighteen months later) had turned the corner and would be okay.

I found myself in another hospital waiting room ten years later. I was nervously awaiting news of my father's open-heart surgery. He and I had been at a pastors' conference in Chicago half-a continent from home when he suffered a near-fatal cardiac arrest in the hotel lobby. The hours waiting for news were made less anxious by friends from the conference who learned of my situation and waited with me. Once again, a positive outcome turned a waiting room into a sanctuary of praise.

As a pastor and a chaplain, I've spent countless hours in hospital waiting rooms helping fearful families shoulder the weight of worry as a loved one is being treated in the ER or undergoing a risky surgical procedure. Sometimes the weight of waiting has given way to tears of joy and hugs of happiness. Other times that weight has resulted in crushing despair, dashed hopes and gut-wrenching sorrow.

Forty-five years of pastoral ministry translates into more trips to area hospitals than I can easily recall. Each waiting room is a little different. And yet each one resembles the other. While the furniture and the artwork vary, what remains the same is the atmosphere of anxiety and anticipation of hope.

But of all the waiting rooms in which I've spent time, the one that has impacted me the most is the waiting room that was large enough for just a few people. It is the room in which my ninety-two-year-old mom died four years ago this month. My brother and I made the decision to place our mother in hospice care following a recent stroke that significantly complicated her decade-long dementia journey. Within days it became obvious that Mom had only days to live. And, thus, the death watch began.

Sitting at her side my brother and I took turns waiting. We held her hand. We swabbed her mouth. We sang over her and prayed for her. All the while we waited. There in that very intimate waiting room, we recalled memories of our mother that signified her significant life. We welcomed extended family members and friends into that miniscule waiting room to wait with us. And in the waiting they found the right moment to say goodbye to someone (now unresponsive) who had influenced their lives in meaningful ways.

Those who have attended someone through the last days of hospice care can likely remember the rollercoaster of emotions that inhabit your vacant soul. You can also attest to toll that waiting takes. And when the end finally does come, you are glad the waiting is over all the while grateful for what the waiting experience allowed for.

With all that in mind, have you ever thought of life as being a waiting room? It quite possibly is the ultimate waiting room. It is where we anticipate the mystery of what yet awaits and where we introspectively brace for the inevitable.

It's true. Life *is* that waiting room where we have the opportunity to acknowledge our need for God and for each other. It is that place where we become more than casual acquaintances with fear, trust, grief and joy. Life is the waiting room where we find the time to sift through what matters from what doesn't. And while time waits for no one, we can (with purpose).

Be Alert to the Beauty Around Us

In last weekend's column, I made reference to having recently been in a hospital waiting room. As you might recall, I was waiting to have blood drawn. I hate to wait, but my patience was aided by what played out before me. It was almost enough to make my blood boil.

Sitting in front of me were no less than eight individuals waiting to be seen by someone. In spite of the fact that there was an incredibly beautiful view beyond the floor-to-ceiling windows, each was glued to their smartphone.

"How dumb can you be?" I thought to myself. "Beyond you is a vista of mountains and trees illuminated by the morning sunshine. And here you are checking your email. Why not slake your thirst for beauty by turning around and drinking it all in?"

Because the irony was too much to ignore, I pulled out my smartphone and took a photo of the view beyond the window and those who were oblivious to it.

What I witnessed reminded me of that wonderful verse by Elizabeth Barrett Browning. *"Earth's crammed with heaven and every common bush afire with God. But only he who sees takes off his shoes. The rest sit round and pluck blackberries."*

Mrs. Browning is alluding to the Old Testament account of Moses encountering the LORD as recorded in the Book of Exodus. What "the prince of Egypt" observes stops him dead in his tracks. When Israel's future leader realized Who it was Who was speaking to him from the burning bush, he recognized he was standing on holy ground.

In direct response to the mystery that captured his imagination, he took off his shoes. What else does one do when gazing into a blazing shrub that does not burn out? What else does one do when acknowledging the source of the mystery in our lives? And so the poet challenges her readers to be alert to the evidence of the Creator's paintbrush on the canvas of creation. She cautions us from being oblivious to the obvious and simply taking the art of living for granted. Reading between Mrs. Browning's poetic lines, I can hear her speak. Can't you? *"Don't be blind to the beauty of the bush. Don't ignore the breadcrumbs that lead to the object of our worship. Don't leave your shoes on. Don't just eat blackberries."*

Dusting for divine fingerprints isn't all that difficult. For after all, according to the poem, *"Earth's crammed with heaven and every bush afire with God..."* There is wonder to behold all around us. There is mystery to ponder every day. The Creator's calling card has been handed to us with hopes we will take note, take time and take off our shoes.

Obviously "taking off our shoes" is a euphemism. It means responding appropriately to the beauty and cosmic signposts in front of us. It means stopping in order to stare. It means pausing in order to ponder. It means worshiping in order to ascribe worth to the One who is worthy of our praise.

And yet I think I know what you're thinking. Does "taking off our shoes" disqualify us from eating the berries from the bush? Does acknowledging God's glory prevent us from enjoying the fruit of His creation? And the answer is a resounding NO!

Wild blackberries grow like topsy where I live on Mercer Island. They are everywhere. And now is the time of the year when those ubiquitous bushes are literally afire with color. They are loaded with plump purple fruit begging to be picked. And I am the designated picker. My wife Wendy is the pie maker. We are a team.

But our annual berry picking regimen begins with the recognition that what we behold and harvest is God's gift to us. Both the growing and the picking are things of beauty to be acknowledged and enjoyed.

And lest you think I'm down on smartphones. I used mine to capture the beauty of where I stopped to picked (having removed my shoes).

Ports-of-Call on an Unforgettable Cruise

I retired from my dream job a few weeks ago. Because the past decade has been like a non-stop vacation, my favorite attire for going to work was an aloha shirt. Those ten trips around the sun have left me with precious memories in the photo album of my mind.

While cleaning out my office, I came across a miniature suitcase on a bookshelf. That tiny piece of luggage was scaled to the American Girl dolls my kids used to play with. It was covered with decals and stickers denoting various ports-of-call. I purchased it in a local thrift store as an object lesson for one of my sermons during the coronavirus outbreak. I glued another decal on the suitcase that simply said COVID-19. It was my less-than-subtle way of illustrating that the global pandemic had taken us on a cruise we'd not soon (if ever) forget.

Although memorable, COVID was a far cry from any tropical trip to the "land of aloha." It resembled more of a non-stop nightmare than a dream vacation. It was like a cruise on the open sea fraught with rogue waves and gale-force winds. Still, that journey we traveled together provided us with a few ports-of-call worthy of remembering.

The first port-of-call was called sheltering-in-place. It was a place we'd not visited previously. We were forced to stay home and stay put. Initially, it felt like being imprisoned. But mandated lockdowns found us taking stock of the value of what we'd previously taken for granted.

We realized how very precious our family members were to us. Having extended time with our spouse and children allowed us the means to focus on their hopes and fears and make note of how the pandemic was impacting them.

Staying at home also caused us to realize how much we enjoyed those with whom we work each day from whom we were temporarily separated. We also acknowledged how much we appreciated the freedom to come and go to our jobs and to the grocery store and to the mall. And even though working from home had its challenges, the flexibility proved meaningful.

Another port-of-call was called the mask mandate. Wearing a cloth or paper mask served as a badge of belonging. It was a means by which we were reminded we were in this fight together. The face mask was a visual aid calling to mind our common humanity. Each of us was affected by an invisible enemy. Each of us was vulnerable. And the mask served to remind us of our need to take precautions for our personal hygiene. Putting on a mask was a prompt to use hand sanitizer as well as to wash our hands (for the length of time it took to sing the Happy Birthday song or the Doxology).

Even though wearing a mask was a nuisance and although we grew weary of staying six feet apart from one another in a public setting, the imposed requirements kept us from becoming apathetic in the face of a virus that took an incalculable toll on people we loved. Masks encouraged us to be alert and take preventative measures for our well-being.

A third port-of-call was called virtual communication. We went ashore with laptops and smart phones in hand. We were tourists in a totally new territory "zooming" here and there and everywhere. We learned how to "do church" while sipping coffee at home in our recliners. We helped our children go to school while sitting at the kitchen table. We Facetimed with family members we couldn't see because of travel restrictions. Microsoft Teams allowed us to both work and worship from home. Virtual meetings became the norm. We did book clubs and prayer groups and choir practice navigating those little squares on our computer screen. Participation from those around-the-world became a possibility unlike any previous time.

Yes, it's true. The ports-of-call on cruise for which we didn't sign up proved to be blessings in disguise. And looking back on that unforgettable journey we call COVID, I think we can honestly say we are grateful for having been there and are better off because of it.

Afternoon Tea with the Galloping Gourmet

When I was a senior in high school, I didn't take home economics. But I wasn't entirely ignorant when it came to the culinary arts. After all, the Galloping Gourmet was on TV every day.

Graham Kerr, was a gourmet chef and entertainer par-excellence. The tall lanky comedic cook with a delightful British accent was fun to watch. He made experimenting in the kitchen fun. How could I have known then that I would be having afternoon tea in his home fifty-five years later?

After learning that Graham was living in a Christian retirement community an hour away, I reached out to him He graciously consented to be interviewed.

On a rainy April afternoon, the sun broke through the clouds as my wife Wendy and I arrived at Warm Beach Senior Community. Graham welcomed us with his signature smile and an invitation to sit down for a cup of tea.

As our eighty-nine year old host, poured our liquid refreshment, I marveled at the miniature plate of healthy nibblies he'd artistically arranged. Toast with homemade huckleberry jam, an Aussie bite, a whole grain biscuit spread with Nutella and a couple slices of watermelon.

Sipping my tea, I asked Graham to reflect on his faith journey. He proceeded to list the various ingredients God had combined that resulted in his spiritual appetite. With the enthusiasm I recalled from his high-energy cooking show, my new friend shared his story.

Graham, an only child, had been raised by well-to-do hoteliers in England. As such he was exposed to the hospitality industry at an early age and learned from master chefs. His meteoric rise to fame came early in his twenties when television came calling in New Zealand and Australia. Soon he was galloping around the globe earning an international reputation. By 1968 *The Galloping Gourmet* debuted on an American network.

Graham told me he was dubbed by the media as "the high-priest of hedonism" because of his playboy persona, his ubiquitous glass of wine and televised entrees bathed in butter and heavy cream. And while his popularity was soaring, his marriage was in free-fall.

While Wendy and I savored our tasty morsels and continued sipping our tea, Graham shared about a near-fatal car accident in 1972 that ended this gourmet's gallop and severely injured his wife. Per a doctor's suggestion, the Kerr's lengthy period of healing included sailing around the world with their three young children on a seventy-one foot yacht.

Within two years, Graham's wife Treena, who had become addicted to pain-killers following the accident, gave her heart to Jesus. Within several months, Graham had followed his wife's lead and gave up the control of his life to a higher power. His surrender resulted in a welcomed release from the success that had held him hostage.

A life of ministry would define the Kerr's new-found freedom. And that ministry included helping people discover a more nutritious way to eat along with modeling for others how to feast on the Word of God through personal Bible study.

Widowed since 2015, Graham initial grief has been replaced by deep gratitude for the life he and Treena shared. That gratitude is fueled by the daily recipe he follows that helps him maintain a nourishing diet of faith. It begins with an hour and a half of Bible study, prayer, meditation and journaling.

Graham proceeded to tell me about the wooden cross that hangs around his neck. He explained that he wears it every day as a reminder of his spiritual identity in Christ. Curiously, it is a cross he carved from one of the spatulas he used in his TV kitchen.

As Wendy and I stood to leave, I noticed the gigantic world map on Graham's living room wall. Anticipating my question, described his current passion. The globe around which he once galloped as a celebrity chef, is a world punctuated by conflict and pain. But it is a world God loves.

Graham wants to facilitate communication with believers in each nation of the world. His desire is to hear what God is doing behind the scenes that isn't making headlines. With the help of other residents in his community, he wants to document a present-day Book of Acts.

Lessons from an Alaska Glacier

On a recent cruise to Alaska, my wife and I spent the better part of one day in Glacier Bay National Park near the village of Hoona. The highlight of the experience for me was photographing Margerie Glacier. This brilliant blue river of ice that flows more than twenty miles from its source in the mountains is some three hundred feet high and stretches a mile from side to side.

I was impressed by what the National Park rangers told us. Although most glaciers in Alaska are receding due to global warming, Margerie Glacier remains quite stable. In fact, it is estimated that Margerie advances about thirty feet a year.

As I pondered the cold facts, I began to reflect on how "secular warming" has impacted our culture. Secularism, by definition, derives its worldview from naturalistic observations devoid of a dependence on the Divine. As such, it overshadows the supernatural and the mystery of a God-centered cosmos. In an expanding secularistic society, the end result is an atmosphere that threatens norms historically based in a Biblically-grounded perspective.

Like most of the glaciers in Alaska, Judeo-Christian values have been noticeably receding the past couple of generations. So, too, has Biblical literacy. If you were to do a survey among elementary children in public schools today, my guess is that most would not be clueless when asked to identify Adam and Eve, David and Goliath or Jonah and the whale.

Several years ago, I was renting a video in a Blockbuster Store. (That in and of itself would indicate just how long ago it was.) Scanning the shelves, a group of high school students chatted among themselves while attempting to find a satirical comedy based on the life of Christ. As they searched for *Life of Brian* by Monty Python, one of the kids attempted to explain what the video was about. "It's about the dude who was born on Christmas!" he explained. "I can't recall his name."

I couldn't believe what I was hearing. This well-educated young man, schooled in one of the best school districts in America, couldn't name the person who was born on Christmas. Furthermore, he didn't realize that the reason we celebrate Christmas to begin with is because of the significance of Jesus' birth.

Since that startling experience twenty years ago, church attendance across our nation has continued to decline. Local churches are closing at an unprecedented rate. In addition, the Bible is no longer assumed to be the authoritative source of supernational revelation. Scripture's time-honored status as the unquestioned and unchanging standard for faith, doctrine and conduct has been replaced by a culture of amoral relativism.

But it's not just changing trends in church attendance and expanded views of Biblical interpretation that sound a cause for alarm. There is a shift in society when it comes to the freedom to practice one's desire to share their personal faith. What we used to call personal evangelism is now labeled proselytizing.

Ironically, the word *evangelism* means "good news." But any attempt to try and extol the virtues of one's faith tradition with an eye towards conversion is now viewed as bad news.

But gratefully there are those who are willing to stand their ground and not cave-in to the boiling influences of society that are melting centuries of tradition and norms. Within the Jewish and Christian communities where I live, minority voices are speaking up about values easily put down by those drumming the cadence of our current culture.

Like the Margerie Glacier, these courageous souls refuse to simply calve off and melt away. But as with that beautiful blue icefield in Glacier Bay, they are an exception to the rule. All the same, their minority voices are needed. We need to be reminded of a rich heritage that is at risk of becoming merely a historical footnote.

Loving Like Jesus

I met a young pastor at the local St. Arbucks twenty years ago this summer. Looking back, I believe our meeting was God-ordained. In that sacred space on holy ground, we pulled a couple chairs together in a corner and created a makeshift confessional. Amid the aroma of freshly brewed coffee, Andrew Thompson confessed a venti-sized dream. I was all ears.

Sipping from a small cup of Pike's Place roast, I spread cream cheese on my bagel and invited my new friend to tell me what was in his heart. The fellowship that followed was nothing less than sweet communion.

This native of Nelson, British Columbia was in the process of moving to Wenatchee. Andrew told me that his goal was to plant a new church. It was his desire to seed hungry hearts with a gospel of hope that would grow into an orchard of spiritual vitality. He would use contemporary music and the arts to communicate the message of Biblical faith in fresh new ways. He knew it would take considerable time to cultivate the ground and prepare the soil. I sensed that his winsome personality and signature smile would go a long way in seeding his dreams.

As I listened, I could tell that this newly minted church planter was wise beyond his years. He had a passion for people. And he wanted to express that passion in intentional ways. Like the Andrew in the Bible who brought his brother Peter to Jesus, this Andrew wanted to share the good news that had changed his life. The approach Andrew verbalized was consistent with a community conversant with the context of bearing fruit. Andrew knew it would take time and he was willing to invest in the process.

The thought of having a Covenant church in the Wenatchee Valley brought a smile to my face. That was the brand of Christianity I had discovered while a student at Seattle Pacific University and with which I had subsequently become affiliated. It was a small relatively unknown denomination that grew out of a renewal movement in the State Lutheran Church in Sweden. As Scandinavians were emigrating to the United States, the seeds of revival came with them.

Although sharing core beliefs with the denomination in which I'd been raised, the Evangelical Covenant Church offered breathing room to think freely to which I was unaccustomed. They baptized infants as well as confessing adults. They held various views on the second coming of Christ and the use of spiritual gifts. While insisting on the authority of Scripture to guide our faith, doctrine and lifestyle, they agreed to disagree on what was considered non-essential doctrine in a spirit of unity.

What Andrew pictured for me the day I met him at Starbucks was a church whose message would be uncomplicated. He wanted to grow a congregation that would attract the spiritually curious by simply loving like Jesus. And, indeed, he has. Over the past two decades I've watched with keen interest as his dream has been realized.

This weekend Columbia Grove Covenant Church celebrates with Pastor Andrew Thompson as he acknowledges the twentieth anniversary of becoming a Covenant pastor and church planter. From its beautiful campus in East Wenatchee, overlooking the Valley it continues to impact, the congregation visualizes its mission to those who drive by. The shrubs that border the church property have been shaped into letters that spell out their ongoing purpose "LOVE LIKE JESUS."

By the way, next February Columbia Grove Covenant Church will celebrate its twentieth anniversary as a congregation.

A Father's Day Reflections

I became a father forty years ago this year. I'll never forget the day. My wife and I were escorted to a labor room and left alone. Standing at Wendy's bedside, my job was to monitor the baby's heartbeat and the frequency of contractions. Depending on the severity of the discomfort, my job was to coach my wife how to breathe relying on the techniques we'd learned in childbirth classes.

Shortly after we settled into a routine that would likely last a few hours, I noticed the baby's heart rate declined dramatically. I was obviously concerned. When the heart rate dropped with every sequential contraction, I raced to find a nurse. Within minutes an emergency c-section was scheduled and all the lessons we'd learned for a natural childbirth went out the window. As Wendy was wheeled into surgery, I'm the one who could have used help remembering how to breathe calmly.

The procedure didn't last all that long, but it seemed like an eternity. When the doctor presented our newborn daughter to me, he explained why the surgery was required. The umbilical cord had become wrapped around our baby's neck and with each contraction it tightened. Had I failed to monitor the monitor, our child could have easily been stillborn.

My first day of fatherhood was my introduction to what being a dad would involve over the next number of years. There is joyful anticipation of an unknown future. There is the need for being coached on how to "breathe" when the "contractions" of daily life take your breath away. There is the realization that normal can give way to abnormal without notice. That happiness can be trumped by fear with no time to brace yourself. In the end the good outweighs the bad.

That first day of fatherhood eliminated any illusion I might have had that my daughter's life (or mine) would be problem-free. I was reminded of that reality four years later when my wife and I dropped Kristin off at her first day of preschool. After leaving our precious firstborn in the care of a stranger, my stomach was in knots. And as we walked to our car in front of the school, I noticed someone had backed into our station wagon leaving significant damage and not leaving a note.

No, a father's life is not without troubles. And neither are the lives of those for which he is privileged to provide and to help guide. We do ourselves a disservice by expecting what isn't realistic. Life becomes less hard when we recognize it is (by definition) difficult. No wonder that time-honored maxim by Robert Browning is this father's mantra. *A man's reach should exceed his grasp or what's a heaven for?*

But lest I end this column on a downer, the overriding emotion I felt that first day of being a dad was one of gratitude and unconditional love. I had reason to be thankful. Kristin was born without complications. She was healthy. She was beautiful. She was mine. I was a proud father who cradled that miniature human being in my arms whenever I could steal her away from my wife.

I know I'm not the first pastor who has compared the love a father has for his child to the love our Heavenly Father has for us. But the firsthand discovery of that truth was so powerful, I was convinced this insight was something unique to me. I truly do understand how much God cares for me by the depth of love I have for my kids. Nothing (underscore nothing) can separate me from them.

"Behold what manner of love the Father has given to us, that *we* should be called children of God. And that is what *we are.*" 1 John 3:1

Playing Church was More Than Just Play

Remember when the neighborhood kids wanted to play army or cowboys and Indians? Sometimes it was "capture the flag" or a pickup game of flag football. Because I wasn't very athletic, I was generally last to be picked when teams were chosen. Still, I went along with what the others had in mind.

When it was my turn to suggest an activity on a Saturday afternoon, however, I suggested a game to which most were unaccustomed. "Let's play church," I said. For a pastor's kid like me, playing church was easy. It didn't require much preparation or equipment. And since my three of my nearby cousins were also pastors' kids, we had a built-in congregation. The others in the neighborhood were invited to join us.

Having watched my pastor-father lead our congregation Sunday after Sunday, I knew how to take an offering. I also knew how to lead the singing. And although my preaching skills were limited to parroting my dad's inflections in the pulpit, I did my best to convert my peers (although most of them knew Jesus as well as I did already).

The clubhouse in the backyard that my dad had constructed with leftover lumber from our home remodel made for a perfect worship space. And into that makeshift sanctuary we did our best to emulate the adults we saw each Sunday morning. "Can I get an amen?" I'd asked. And without exception, I always did.

In addition to emulating the order of a typical worship service, I'd also conduct funerals for dead birds or squirrels. I would pray over the lifeless critters and then we'd bury them in a Folgers coffee can or a cigar box. Even at the tender age of ten, I felt a sense of mystery around a living creature that had lost its ability to chirp or scurry.

Looking back on those days of pretending, I think I know why I wanted to play church instead of kick-the-can or tag. It was because church was important to me. The church felt like my second home. The people my parents' age (and those old enough to be my grandparents) called me by name. They affirmed me. They told me they were praying for me.

What is more, even though he was the pastor, my dad was never too busy to welcome me into his office. I have a photo of me as a three-year-old sitting at the typewriter where he'd type his sermon outlines. He allowed me to enter his world. As such, I felt comfortable in that holy place where God encountered my dad with a message to share with his flock.

I would often visit my dad after school. While he was engaged in sermon preparation or typing the Sunday bulletin on a stencil, I would stand behind the pulpit in the sanctuary and engage an invisible audience. Dad didn't mind that I pretended that sacred desk was a podium in the East Wing of the White House. Since John Kennedy was President at the time, I imagined myself as JFK at one of his frequent televised press conferences. I even did my best to impersonate President Kennedy's Bostonian accent.

Playing church or pretending to be the President proved to be more than child's play. It was in my father's church that I began to feel a call to fulltime ministry. I felt at home in the church and on the platform and in the pastor's study. I felt at home with God's people.

Going through the motions in my youth was a means by which the Lord began to prepare me for what would be my vocation for forty-five years and counting. I credit a loving dad whose persona through the week was the same as his persona on Sundays. Whereas many preachers' kids (PKs) I've known rebelled from their religious roots as they entered adolescence, I did not. I was grateful for the privilege of being raised in a pastor's family and in the home of one who didn't object to me playing church in the backyard.

Words to the Wise!

It's that time of year again! In a nation that continually looks across the pond for its royalty fix, we have our annual opportunity to embrace a regal atmosphere of ceremonial ritual.

Although they are a far cry from a king's coronation, graduation ceremonies allow us to feel a sense of pomp amid our circumstances. There is a certain splendor in the ritual that crowns the achievement of those who have reached an educational milestone.

Part of the pomp is the keynote address given to the graduates. That challenge typically is a laundry list of life lessons reminding the class of gowned and capped achievers what to "sort," when to "bleach," how to "hand wash" and what to "hang dry" in order to maximize results.

For college commencements, speakers are typically celebrity guests from off campus. For high school graduations, the speakers tend to be students who have excelled academically. In both instances, the retention reality of what is shared remains a bit suspect. Continuing the "laundry list" metaphor, what was said in a commencement address is easily "lost in the wash."

Upon reflection, after a half-century since I donned my cap and gown, I would like to pose an idea for administrators to ponder as future ceremonies are planned. Why not choose a beloved teacher who has a personal relationship with the graduating class? Perhaps their time-tested advice for a successful future might prove more colorfast. It just might have more of a "cling factor." Let me offer an example.

Even though Pershing Beglau was not invited to address our graduating class in the spring of 1970, what he taught me four years earlier left a permanent crease in the fabric of my character. This man, with the rather unusual name, was my 8th grade social studies teacher at Pioneer Junior High. His knit neckties with the squared-off tail conveyed the seriousness with which he viewed his vocation. He modeled decorum and decency.

He introduced me to classical music I'd never heard at home. As we entered his classroom, Mr. Beglau's penchant for flamenco guitar music was evident. Records by Carlos Montoya were played regularly. The enthusiasm with which he shared his musical passion rubbed off. I am a classical music lover to this day. In fact, I still have the Carlos Montoya album I bought in in 1965 to be like Mr. B.

And it was Mr. Beglau who first inspired me to write for a newspaper. (And I still am writing for one.) Our class published a paper we called "The World Scene." That weekly rag included paraphrased articles summarizing current events we were studying as well as a political cartoon. And speaking of political cartoons, it was Mr. Beglau who taught us how to make not of them and understand their meaning. Every Monday we had to turn in a cartoon with an explanation of what the cartoonist was attempting to day.

How I wish Mr. Beglau had been chosen to address our senior class. I'm quite sure his words would have had staying power. The relationship we had with him (and he with us) would have guaranteed that. And yet, even though that was not the case, there was something Mr. B shared with us in the eighth grade that had a valedictorian punch to it. All these years later, I still remember what he scrawled with a piece of white chalk on the blackboard…

"He who knows not and knows not he knows not: he is a fool - shun him. He who knows not and knows he knows not: he is simple - teach him. He who knows and knows not he knows: he is asleep - wake him. He who knows and knows he knows: he is wise - follow him."

Now if that isn't wrinkle-free wisdom, I don't know what is.

A Tale of Two Elsies

As we observe Mother's Day once again this year, I'm mindful of a mother by the name of Elsie. That was the name her parents chose when she was born ninety-six years ago.

Barely five feet tall, Elsie was a giant in the lives of her two sons. She embraced motherhood with tiptoe enthusiasm. Her creative flair and hands-on joie d-vie left her mark on her family and all who knew her. Having had an amazing mother herself, this mom took her cues from one who had quit school in third grade to help care for her eleven younger siblings on a farm in Kitsap County.

Elsie's mother had taught herself how to play the guitar, piano and harmonica. She was a gifted artist and vocalist. She modeled compassion and nurture. She guided her three children in the ways of the Lord. Since Elsie was her youngest, the baby of the brood was the recipient of her mother's focused attention.

As she entered adolescence, Elsie resisted being called by the name her parents chose for her. That was about the time that the mascot of Borden Milk Company was a cow by the name of Elsie. For a petite pretty blonde to be called by a bovine's name was "udderly" embarrassing. So, when she entered high school Elsie began to go by her middle name.

Following college, Elsie met a young Greek American who was the pastor of a small church in the panhandle of Idaho. After a dozen dates, they became engaged and were married in January of 1951. She became a mom fifteen months later.

And then there was another mother by the name of Elsie. This Elsie became a mother in 1931. Unlike the other Elsie, this Elsie did not have the godly example of a nurturing parent. Longing for love, found herself in the unenviable situation of being pregnant without the benefit of being married.

As a nineteen-year-old, Elsie chose not to abort the child within her. Valuing the miniature life she was carrying, she gave birth to a baby boy. She attempted to keep her son, but soon discovered the demands of caring for the child on her own were beyond her ability. Elsie made the courageous decision to give up her little one to the Children's Aid Society of Vancouver when the boy (whom she named Hugh) was only six months old.

Elsie never saw her baby again. While she would eventually marry and have three other children, she died without knowledge of what had become of her firstborn. While she assumed her son would be adopted, she could never have imagined the life he would lead.

Following his education and beginning a career track with a major department store chain, Elsie's son married and began a family of his own. A call to cross-cultural missions found the young husband and father living in Mexico City where he discovered his abilities as a writer.

Fifty books (and countless magazine articles) later, Elsie's son, now ninety-two lives in Southern California with his wife of seventy-two years. He has recently written his memoir in which he includes a letter he wrote to a mother he never knew.

This man has shared with me the angst with which he has lived having been denied a relationship with his birth mom. After all, I married his firstborn daughter.

And in case you're wondering, I knew the first Elsie mentioned in this story as well. The middle name by which she chose to go by was Star. And she was the guiding star of my life from the time she gave me birth seventy-one years ago until she died four years ago

A Preview of Coming Attractions

While the eyes of much of the world are on London this weekend, residents of the Wenatchee Valley are focused on events surrounding the 104th Apple Blossom Festival. The coronation of King Charles is a newsworthy event to be sure, but so, too, is the reign of Queen Scarlette and her two princesses.

I experienced my very first Apple Blossom Festival when I was thirteen. It was a highlight of the year for a new kid in town. Cradling my E-flat alto saxophone in my arms, I marched in the Kids Parade as part of the Pioneer Junior High School Band. Being part of an all-city event was a thrill.

In high school I got to be involved in festivities surrounding the selection of the royalty. As a senior I even had the enviable privilege of dating the Apple Blossom Queen. To this day memories of the Meeker carnival rides and attractions are still triggered this time of year.

One of the fondest memories I have of the festival was of a much more serious nature. It occurred the first weekend in May in 1972. That was the year recording artist Pat Boone was the headliner at an ecumenical worship gathering in the Apple Bowl.

Because I was on the editorial staff of my college newspaper, I was invited to a breakfast with Pat Boone at the home of Paul and Kay Pugh prior to the community-wide celebration. I got to pose questions to the entertainer widely known for his penchant of wearing white shoes. The tanned celebrity was most cordial to this novice interviewer.

But the most impressive memory of that weekend was the worship service itself. The football stadium stands on both sides of the field were filled. A capacity crowd sitting on folding chairs covered the gridiron. As Pat Boone sang praises to God and spoke of his personal faith journey, the audience listened in rapped attention. I was one of those drinking it all in. As a kid who listened to my parents' music, I'd been a Pat Boone fan for years. His "April Love" was most welcomed on this warm May morning.

The audience that morning was comprised of those who had followed the crooner's career from the time they were teenagers as well as current teenagers who hadn't a clue who Pat Boone was. In addition to the wide spectrum of ages, there was an equally diverse denominational representation. Attendees included those from the local Catholic, Lutheran, Episcopal and Methodist churches as well as those from less liturgical congregations like the Baptists, Evangelicals and Charismatics.

Looking back on that combined gathering of Christ followers, I can see that I was being given a preview of coming attractions. Half a century ago I had a sneak peek at what the Scripture says will one day be the norm. There is coming a time when doctrinal differences and divisions that currently separate the faithful will give way to unity and cooperation. The young and those older, no matter their skin color, culture or language will come together and join in a unison chorus of praise to the Creator.

What I experienced that Apple Blossom Festival weekend was the indication of what lies in store. And how appropriate that it would happen while valley orchards were boasting their beautiful blossoms. Just as apple blossoms on a tree are a precursor of the fruit that will be harvested come fall, so too are examples of Christian unity wherever we see them. An amazing harvest awaits!

Minding Your '*p*'s and '*q*'s

Have you ever wondered where the old expression *mind your 'p's and 'q's* came from? There are various suggestions as to the origin of the phrase. Some refer to the similarity of moveable type used in old-time printing presses where the letter *'p'* and the letter *'q'* could easily be mistaken. Another explanation has to do with teaching children how to write lower-case 'p's and 'q's beginning with an circle shape and then adding a descending line either from the left for *'p'* or the right for *'q.'* No matter the correct explanation, the expression means "watch what you're doing" or "be on your best behavior."

I learned to mind my *'p'*s and *'q'*s by working at KPQ during my senior year at Wenatchee High School. As you may recall, back in the sixties our hometown radio station was one of the first fully automated stations in the country. Large eighteen-inch reels of prerecorded music from IGM (International Good Music) were operated by early computers. My job consisted of giving live station IDs at the top of the hour and announcing the time and temperature before putting ABC Network News on-the-air.

But a large part of each shift included processing IBM cards through the punch machine to code the rectangle-shaped cards. Depending on how they were coded, the cards (when loaded in the computer) would activate the large tapes to play a music selection or trigger a carousel-like apparatus filled with 8-track style cassettes so that a commercial would be played.

Perhaps you remember the names of Don McMaster and Del Olney who were the automated announcers introducing the easy-listening music that had been prerecorded at IGM's studios in Bellingham. And then there was another favorite deejay. Remember Doug Pledger?

So what does all that radio nostalgia have to do with learning to mind my 'p's and 'q's? Well, *u c* it's like this. Since my weekend shift was typically 6pm to 6am, I ordinarily brought a midnight snack to feed my overnight hunger. But one night around 3am in the morning, I decided to live dangerously. Even though I knew that I was under no circumstances to leave the premises, I figured *"What the heck! The computer cards are fully stacked. The music will play without interruption for a couple hours. Why can't I drive down Wenatchee Avenue to the Denny's and have a Grand Slam Breakfast? I'd be back in forty-five minutes easy."*

To play it safe, I took a portable radio with me as I drank coffee and scarfed down my eggs, bacon and pancakes at the counter. But before I could finish, I noticed the music on *AM 560* gave way to absolute silence. KPQ was off-the-air. Something had gone wrong with the automation. And I was not in the studio.

I hurriedly paid my bill and raced back to the station only to field a call from my irate boss, the station manager, Jim Wallace. (Why he was listening at 3am I never did discover.) I had not minded my '*p*'s and '*q*'s and I had been caught. *o g* was I in trouble. If you figured that was the last time I attempted such a high-risk escapade, *u r* absolutely correct.

In retrospect, I should have known. There is a verse in the Old Testament (Numbers 32:23) that I memorized as a child without much effort. It was because of the number of times I heard my parents remind me of it. *"Be sure your sins will find you out."* In other words, wrong choices we make eventually come to light. Jesus made a similar observation. *"For there is nothing covered that will not be revealed, nor hidden that will not be known."* (Luke 12:2)

And there is one other verse in the Bible that I've contemplated much. While my three daughters were learning their ABCs, it reminded of my responsibility to help my girls mind their 'p's and 'q's. Proverbs 22:6 says, *"Train up a child in the way they should go and when they are old they will not depart from it."* And believe it or not, part of that training involves acknowledging our missteps along the way.

Poetry is My Bag

April is National Poetry Month. However, I celebrate poetry every month of the year. I have a rhyme for most every reason. I've written four books of poetry. I have a syndicated poetry blog for which I publish verse weekly. And truth be told, I write a rhyme of some kind most every day. Someone once suggested that my mind thinks in iambic pentameter.

The first poem I remember composing was for Mrs. Hendricks second grade class at Liberty Elementary School in Marysville. But my fascination with poetry really took off in high school and college. I wrote romantic lyrics for the girls I was dating. And I wrote parodies of classic poems in an attempt to impress my literature professor. Prior to Dr. Erickson's lectures, I would arrive early to write a poem on the blackboard that would greet my classmates when they arrived. I gained a reputation for my wit and creativity. While escorting tours to Alaska and the Canadian Rockies during summer vacations, my penchant for writing humorous lyrics served me well. I wrote poetry for our farewell dinners.

Fast-forward fifty years. When COVID altered our lifestyles, new phrases like "sheltering in place" and "socially distancing" became incorporated into our daily parlance. We masked-up before going-out in addition to learning the importance of applying hand sanitizing gel throughout the day. Lockdowns limited our normal activities. But gratefully walking outside was never forbidden. As a result, my wife and I walked several times a week. In addition to being good for our hearts, it was good for our minds.

Enter Pioneer Park. Near to where Wendy and I live is an expansive forest of evergreen trees and well-maintained trails. When COVID first invaded, I would discover beautifully hand-painted rocks hidden on our walking path. It was like going on an Easter egg hunt. The stones were barely visible in the hollow of a decaying tree, at the base of a tree trunk or perched on a bench.

These commemorative stones typically included slogans like... *"Keep calm and socially distance!" "Breathe!" "You are loved!"* and *"Hope!"* They were brief sentiments that invited passersby to walk on and look up. Sometimes the rocks offered a miniature portrait of a sunset or happy face.

And then it hit me. Even though I am not artistic with a brush, I love to paint word pictures. Why not pen a brief rhyme or an upbeat slogan on a brown paper bag and tack it to a tree on the trail? Hearing no objections, that's exactly what I started to do. That was three years ago. And I am still doing it.

My most recent paper bag poem looks back on the pandemic in past tense. It simply says *"What COVID stole left us sick but didn't leave us poor."* Like many of my lunch bag offerings, it doesn't actually rhyme. So, I guess you'd call them blank verse. All the same they are portraits on what is known as the poet tree.

Although I have attempted to keep my contributions anonymous, I've been caught a few times tacking a new poem to the tree. And now I've decided to publish the past three-years of poems in a volume. Since my name will be on the cover, the bard of the forest won't be anonymous any longer. The book's rather unimaginative title is *Paper Bag Poems in Pioneer Park*. But the subtitle offers a clue to its practical use. *An Interactive Walking Journal.*

My hope is that the photos of the poems will inspire personal contemplation about how the message is applicable to those who read them. A blank page adjacent to each photo will provide space for the intended purpose of journaling ideas, resolutions, goals or tracking miles walked on any given day.

A Mane Metaphor for the Almighty

Lions are not limited to making an appearance in just one section of the Bible. In the Old Testament as Abraham's grandson Jacob is dying, he offers a blessing to his twelve sons. When he gets to Judah, he likens him to a courageous lion. And then there is the terrifying scenario where the prophet Daniel finds himself sentenced to the den of a ferocious lion. And, of course, there is the reference to the Messianic Kingdom when the wolf will lie down with the lamb and the lion and the calf will peacefully co-exist.

Fast-forward then to the New Testament and we see the Apostle Peter comparing Satan to a prowling lion who stealthily attempts to devour godly individuals. And in the Book of Revelation the lion is once again seen as a positive metaphor for the reigning Messiah.

There is something about lions that fascinate me. From the first time I saw one at Woodland Park Zoo as a kid to watching the iconic lion roaring at the start of an MGM film, I continue to be awed by the power and majesty the king of the beast embodies. And recently I find myself thinking a lot about lions. And the "mane" reason dates back some fifty years.

This month my college roommate, an expert on the life and work of C.S. Lewis, is sharing his knowledge for the benefit of the residents of the senior adult community where I work. For more than four decades Kim Gilnett has studied Lewis' life and his extensive writings. Kim has even traveled to Oxford England to participate in the restoration of the famed author's home. After recently watching Shadowlands, where

Anthony Hopkins portrays Lewis, I've envied Kim's unique opportunities.

In one of his first lectures Kim referenced the books that Lewis wrote primarily for children. The *Chronicles of Narnia* offers spiritual lessons through the creative use of fantasy and allegory. Aslan, the lion character in the chronicles, bears a strong resemblance to the personality and actions of Jesus Christ.

Aslan has long fascinated me as an approachable Christ-like image. One who, according to C.S. Lewis, is good but hardly safe. Perhaps that was in the back of my mind when I wrote a book about the presence of Aslan in our twenty-first century lives.

In *When God Speaks: Listening for Aslan in Everyday Life*, I make a case for the fact that the Creator continues to interact with His creation. Much like the fictional lion in Lewis' chronicles, I see the Almighty as both frightening and kind. God is all-powerful and all-knowing all the while intent on being in relationship with fallible and flawed individuals. Thus, Christians, who have just celebrated Easter, understand the incarnation of the Creator in the person of Jesus. For Christ-followers, a belief in the first century rabbi's resurrection includes finds us aware of his continuing (albeit unseen) presence. Like Aslan, he is uncage-able as well as being approachable.

I keep a miniature stone lion on my desk at work. My personal Alsan reminds me of a God that is both unlike me, but like me at the same time. And I recently discovered I'm not the only one helped by such tangible symbolism. A resident at The Shores has an extensive collection of Aslans that Char has graciously agreed to display during our month-long C.S. Lewis emphasis. For her, the lion image is a powerful picture of strength for times in our lives when we find ourselves acknowledging our weakness. This *mane* metaphor for the Almighty is something with which children of all ages can identify.

By the Dawn's Early Light

The grandfather clock in the hallway had just chimed midnight. When the hearse arrived two hours later, a steady rain was falling in the darkness.

I stood on the front porch of our home on Gellatly Street and watched the funeral director wheel the shroud-covered body of my pastor-father to the waiting car. Through a veil of tears, I watched the black mini-van drive away.

That night I also watched for the dawn. More than ever, I wanted the darkness of night to dissolve into day. While a new day technically begins at midnight, dawn provides the tangible evidence that morning has broken. My broken heart longed for a new day that might help distance me from my grief.

There's something powerful about the dawning of a new day. I often think of the psalmist who chronicled his own longing for dawn: *"Weeping may linger for the night, but joy comes with the morning..."* (Psalm 30:5 NRSV)

In addition, the dawn's early light was obviously meaningful to the poet who penned the lyrics to our national anthem. Francis Scott Key celebrated a victorious defense of Fort Mc Henry as he welcomed a new day. First light also proved holy to the women who found Jesus' grave empty on the first day of the week. Dawn revealed a reason for hope.

As I contemplated my dad's death that cold and rainy November night, the approaching dawn was more than a predictable reality. The coming light represented the means by which I could see to navigate a new norm. Life without my dad would be difficult but I realized the separation would only be temporary. The first light of that first Easter guaranteed that.

Ironically, one of my favorite memories of my dad relates to an experience I shared with him on an Easter morning. When I was ten years old, my dad asked if I would help him distribute bulletins at an Easter sunrise service. He was one of the pastors participating in the community-wide ecumenical gathering. I reluctantly agreed.

Dad woke me up 0-dark-thirty. I dressed warmly and gulped down a glass of orange juice before we headed out the door. As my father drove us to the high school football stadium in the dark, I wiped the sleep from my eyes.

Why did I agree to do this? I hate getting up early, I thought to myself as I shivered in the cold. But as we took our places at the entrance to the stadium, I discovered the reason.

The dark sky began to brighten. I proudly stood beside my dad and followed his lead passing out programs. Triumphant music began to play in the background. My heart began to beat faster as the sun rose higher above the horizon.

It was the first time in my life I recalled having seen a sunrise. My reluctance of crawling out of bed in the dead of night was replaced by an incredible rush of joy.

Until the death of my father, I'd loved sunrises but had never been much of a morning person. But the night he died was a turning point for me. Something in me shifted, and I became much more drawn to the dawn.

There's something about daybreak that I have come to embrace. Just as Jesus' disciples associated dawn with death's defeat, so now do I.

I have also come to see that dawn is a mysterious moment when my perspective is calibrated. The regrets of yesterday succumb to the expectations of a new day.

Each day, life begins anew. With each new sunrise, I have the chance to dance with new possibilities and refocus my gaze on what faith promises. By the dawn's early light, I sense the presence of a holy God. In the light of a new day, I feel fully alive.

Graceland or Grazeland

Where were you when you learned of Elvis death? I was at the Mendenhall Glacier Visitor Center near Juneau, Alaska escorting a group of senior adults. Like JFK's assassination, the first moon landing and 9/11, such memorable events are engraved on our memory.

Elvis may have left the building for the last time forty-six years ago, but he is still very much a part of our lives. The recent blockbuster movie about "The King" has contributed to that fact. The buzz at both the Golden Globes and Academy Awards was noteworthy.

A couple months ago, my wife and I saw "Elvis" on the big screen at our local theatre. The soundtrack brought back so many memories of my teenage years. I watched the film for the second time on a flight while recently traveling to Tampa for a weekend of speaking engagements.

Ironically, about the time we were passing over Memphis, I was transfixed by the tragic consequences of a talented life projected on the miniature monitor embedded in the seat back in front of me. Elvis' roots irrigated in Tupelo and Memphis produced a harvest of fame that sadly grew among the weeds of drug addiction which eventually choked out his career.

For such a troubled life, Elvis' Pentecostal upbringing and early exposure to God's love must have provided him a security blanket of sorts. Perhaps that's why he named the white pillared mansion he bought for his parents "Graceland." Like much of the other details in the film, the portrayal of this celebrated estate was extremely realistic.

It convinced me I needed to add a visit to Graceland to my bucket list of places to see.

For a man of the cloth whose worldview is woven with the fabric of faith, something called Graceland calls to mind much more than just a must-see landmark in Memphis. For me the name Graceland suggests an atmosphere where grace is embraced with intentionality and gratitude. It's a realm in which forgiveness and fresh starts comprise the air we breathe. Graceland is the territory of trust I believe the Creator created for His creatures to inhabit.

For those who follow the Christian faith, grace is revealed in the New Testament as the means by which we obtain right standing with God and the promise of eternal life. As we approach Good Friday, the message of that day reminds us that grace is the antithesis of trying to earn God's favor by working hard at being good. Grace is the offer we are given by which we can freely benefit from someone else's good work. It is the privilege to use another person's credit to pay-off what we owe.

After arriving in Florida on my recent flight, I noticed a street sign in the Sarasota neighborhood where I was staying. I did a double take. From a distance the sign appeared to say GRACELAND. But as I looked more closely it read GRAZELAND.

Again, my always-looking-for-a-good-sermon-illustration radar detector began to flash with insight. It occurred to me that Grazeland is where most Christ-followers I know tend to live. Rather than putting down roots in Graceland (and acknowledging complete dependence on the Divine's offer), they tend to nibble at the concept of unconditional love and graze at the edges of grace.

Given the do-it-yourself culture in which we were raised, we are taught to pull our own weight and not be owing to anybody. As a result, grace is often held at arms-length. We say we are grateful for God's grace but live as though it doesn't exist. Perhaps it's our way of playing it safe.

Holy Week provides Christians an opportunity to revisit the central message of their faith and determine if they are currently living in the city limits of Graceland or Grazeland.

Prayer: A Capitol Idea

The first prayer I ever offered before state legislators was in Springfield, Illinois a couple decades ago.

A close friend who served in the Illinois State Senate invited me to make the three-hour drive from our home in suburban Chicago. It was a distinct honor and rare privilege to see where a young legislator by the name of Abraham Lincoln got his political start.

As best as I can determine, another young legislator who would also become President of the United States was in that room that morning. As Barak Obama sat at his desk, I stood at the podium and gave my prayer. As I basked in the glow of that special moment, I had no idea that would be the first of many opportunities I would have to pray before a group of lawmakers.

After moving to Washington in 2005, I've made several trips to Olympia to pray before the State Senate or the State House of Representatives. I always consider it an honor to lead our state politicians in a moment of focus in which they recognize their accountability before and dependence on the Almighty.

If ever there was a time when political divisions and culture wars called for a sacred time out, it is in this conflicted season of history. Just this week I was invited to begin the daily proceedings in the state legislature with an opening prayer. What follows is the text of what I prayed…

Good morning, Creator God,
On this first day of spring
would you teach us to sing with the songbirds?

Their melodic chirping celebrates the promise
of new beginnings that are characterized
by the colorful blooms that push
their beauty above ground to display Your glory.
What an awesome God You are!

This morning we also celebrate
the diversity of color and culture
that characterizes our Evergreen State.
We are grateful for the garden of humanity
of which we are a part
and that which you've called us to tend on Your behalf.

And now as daylight increasingly invades
the evening hours, would You illuminate
the understanding of these in this chamber
who seek to improve the conditions of our citizens.
May compromise and cooperation prevail
in caucuses and general sessions alike.

Holy and loving God, may a common pursuit
of law and order as well as justice and mercy
motivate these who reach across the aisle to govern.

As the warmth of spring sunshine
encourages the germination and growth
of all that beautifies the landscape of our lives,
may the warmth of genuine friendship
result in a lingering fragrance and lasting beauty
that draws us together for the common good.
For it is in Your name we pray. Amen.

Celebrating the Oscars in Our Lives

Last Sunday Hollywood honored its own with the 95th Academy Awards Ceremony. As is our family custom, we decorated the fireplace mantel with movie memorabilia. From the time our kids were little, we would use Oscar Night as an opportunity to dress up, eat a nice dinner and then watch the televised ceremonies as a family while scoring our individual ballots. Now that our three daughters are grown, Wendy and I have simplified our tradition. But we still decorate the mantel and watch the ceremonies with ballots in hand.

Recently, I got to wondering how the little gold statue awarded to Academy winners got the nickname Oscar. Turns out there are three plausible explanations. One version suggests that the name originated with Margaret Herrick, a former Academy librarian, who insisted that the silhouette of the trophy resembled her Uncle Oscar. If that's the case, her relatively unknown family member has left a lasting shadow on an industry of which he was not a part.

I had an Uncle Oscar. Maybe you did, too. But my grandmother's youngest brother isn't the only Oscar who has paraded across the stage of my life. There was Oscar Nelson with whom I went to high school. Nellie was a gifted athlete! There was Oskar Schindler whose famous life-saving list inspired a movie that impacted me deeply. I will never forget laying a stone at his grave in Jerusalem to symbolize my gratitude for his life.

There was Oscar de la Renta whose overpriced dress shoes I purchased at a thrift store in Napa, California the same day that I wore them for my best friend's wedding. And there's little Oscar Anderson. He's the five-year-old grandson of good friends from Illinois I have yet to meet in person. (Thank God for Facebook!) And, of course, there's Oscar the Grouch from Sesame Street who intersected our kids' lives long before they knew about the Academy Awards or Facebook.

Except for the grouchy one who lives in a trash can, the Oscars in my life are real people with real stories of struggles and challenges as well as being loved and being given opportunities to love. For them learning their lines is a daily occurrence. Except for those who have taken their final curtain call, the script of these Oscars' lives is still in the process of being written. It is not the product of a screenwriter.

The same is true with regard to your script and mine. Each day we act and react in accordance to the circumstances we randomly encounter for which we cannot prepare. Each day we are presented with a chance to offer the performance of our lives. But the script is of our own making.

Although we do not have a predetermined script, we are not left on our own. As a person of faith, I affirm the presence of Someone who is involved in "the dailies" of the movie that is my life. I believe there is Someone in the director's chair who provides me with cues for what I should do and what I should say or when I should remain silent on the soundstage of daily living. That's how I understand my Creator. Ours is a God who coaches from the sidelines. And the eventual reward we are promised for acting on the cues we've been given is "out of this world." Based on what I read in Scripture, it's even better than the Oscars Hollywood hands out.

And speaking of the Oscars, have you ever contemplated the irony of that little gold man? Those who win one are rewarded for pretending to be someone other than who they really are. That's the nature of acting. As much as I'd enjoy having an authentic Oscar on my fireplace mantel, I'll likely never get one. But I'm okay with that.

As far as I'm concerned, being a productive performer in the drama of daily life is much more meaningful and accessible than the pretense of a scripted and costumed role. Each day you and I are invited to celebrate being ourself and making a difference in the world in the process.

A Time for Jesus

It was a time for Jesus! Literally it was. I still have the *Time* magazine cover from June 21, 1971. There was something about that psychedelic image that arrested my teenage attention. The cover story was all about the Jesus revolution in our culture. Something remarkable was happening in our country back then.

Against the backdrop of racial turmoil, protests of an unpopular war and the hippie culture marked by drugs, sex and rock-n-roll, a spiritual awakening was taking place. Long-haired rebels were beginning to keep short accounts with God. And the Wenatchee Valley was not exempt.

I was a teenager at the time and have vivid memories of that unforgettable season. A couple years prior to the Time magazine issue, there were stirrings of faith. It was felt in our local schools. Our Christian club at Wenatchee High School was called *Revolution for Christ* or "RFC." That home-grown Christian group led by students met in the choir room over lunch. Attendance grew among churched kids and those who were curious. It was exciting!

Meanwhile, a twenty-something pastor and his wife moved to town from California. Larry and Devi Titus began to minister to a fringe group of teens in the city parks. Those who had been high on pot became high on Jesus. What emerged was a growing revival in the valley.

It included a half-way house for runaways and those who were spiritually seeking. *The House of Mercy* was a gathering place for Bible study, worship and recovery. A café opened on Orondo Street called *Good Sam's*. A Christian radio station on Wenatchee Avenue was launched.

Most notably, the old Monitor school became home to the growing church and an eventual Bible college. Critics (justifiably concerned about mismanagement of the movement) were outnumbered by those being genuinely converted.

About the same time a small church in Costa Mesa, California by the name of Calvary Chapel was experiencing exponential growth. Pastor Chuck Smith served as a spiritual labor-and-delivery physician as countless hippies were "born again." *Free Love* decals gave way to *Honk if You Love Jesus* bumper stickers.

Simultaneously, a Southern California writer by the name of Hugh Steven wrote a book documenting the unprecedented happenings as they were unfolding. In *The Reproducers,* Steven refers to nineteen-year old Greg Laurie who responded to the acceptance and hope he'd been denied in his dysfunctional family. It's a story that lays the foundation for what millions of Americans are currently flocking to theatres to see.

The popular film *Jesus Revolution* is based on Greg Laurie's autobiography and describes how the Jesus People movement of the late sixties and early seventies catapulted him from a drug-using loser to a successful high-respected pastor.

As I watched the movie, I was immersed with memories from a half-century ago. What I saw on the big screen triggered a confidence that lives of disenchanted and marginalized people we know can find healing and transformation. Scenes of those being baptized in the Pacific Ocean recalled a simpler time when public affirmation of one's faith was not limited to a stained-glass sanctuary. I wondered if it could happen again.

Amazingly, the *Time* magazine cover that I saved actually factors into the movie. The reporter who wrote the cover story for that 1971 issue is woven into the script.

And get this. At the same time the *Time* correspondent was researching his story, the author of the *The Reproducers* was collecting material and taking photos of the Calvary Chapel explosion. His oldest child witnessed the phenomenon in person. She worshipped in the huge circus tent that served as a church building. She attended concerts of Christians bands that were birthed out of that movement.

As she left the theater after seeing *Jesus Revolution*, Hugh's daughter commented just how accurate the movie was to what she experienced. I heard her comments as I walked her to the car. You see, I married the daughter of the guy who wrote the original history of the Jesus movement. Hugh Steven is Wendy Asimakoupoulos' father.

Hail to the Chiefs

"Hail to the Chiefs!" No, I'm not referring to the Super Bowl victory parade in Kansas City this past week. But that was some celebration, wasn't it?

And while we're on that topic... In spite of the fact that one of the residents at the senior adult community where I work was a coach for the Chiefs, I actually was hoping for an Eagles win. (No, I won't confess my bias to Coach Brasher!)

But my three-year-old granddaughter put it all into perspective. Little Ivy came to our Super Bowl party wearing her Seahawks shirt. It was so great! I took her photo and posted it on my Facebook page. My caption indicated that our family gathering was a dress rehearsal for next year's big game. Let's hope so! Go Hawks!

Actually, my reference to "Hail to the Chiefs!" is a recognition that this is Presidents Day Weekend! Monday is a federal holiday. It's a day in which we are invited to reflect on all the inhabitants of the White House and recognize their contributions to our lives, liberties and the pursuit of our happiness. Truth be told (Honest Abe), some are more deserving of reflection than others.

Back when I was a kid, we recognized both Abraham Lincoln's birthday (February 12) and George Washington's birthday (February 22) in school. Do you remember when we combined the two birthday observances into one? That answer might serve you well if you're ever on Jeopardy. It was on June 28, 1968 when Congress passed the Uniform Monday Holiday Act which consolidated the two birthdays into Presidents Day.

More information that you wanted to know? I get it. We live in a world where we are inundated with too much information. Twenty-four-hour cable news. Breaking news alerts on our smart phones. Emails that accrue on every device we own. Endless threads that populate on our Facebook posts. Continual texts. There are just way too many words that dominate our lives.

Too often we contribute to an out-of-control cacophony of words by unnecessarily joining the chorus of those around us. Maybe you were like I was during class discussions in college. Even if I didn't understand what was being discussed, I felt the need to speak up. After all, I didn't want to be considered stupid. Sadly, I didn't appreciate the value of simply listening. Unfortunately, I didn't understand the importance of silence. I also didn't understand that pontificating prematurely can expose one's lack of understanding.

On this Presidents Day Weekend, there is a quote that may well have originated in the White House. It's a quote that speaks to our word-saturated culture. It's a quote attributed to Lincoln that says, *"Better to keep your mouth shut and be thought a fool than to open it and remove all doubt."*

Although there is some doubt as to whether our sixteen President actually said them, those nineteen words pack quite a punch. The give cause for pause. Do I really need to respond to what I've just heard? Would it be okay to just listen? Would a day of reflecting on that with which I initially disagree allow me to speak with more intelligence and empathy tomorrow? Could my choice of remaining silent start a chain reaction of less talk and less opinion?

Although I haven't been able to find a definitive answer as to who originally spoke the words "about words" attributed to Lincoln, what I have found is most insightful. A axiom very much like the Lincoln quotation is credited to a king and not a President. The original version comes from King Solomon and is recorded in the Old Testament.

In Proverbs 17:29 it says, *"Even fools are thought wise if they keep silent and discerning if they hold their tongues."* 'Nuff said?

Memories of a Sad Day and an Unforgettable Poem

Last weekend a sad anniversary in our nation's history was overshadowed by the release of the video that captured the beating of Tyre Nichols. The five former Memphis police officers who were charged in the unarmed motorist's subsequent death took precedence over the seven Challenger astronauts who perished in a Space Shuttle launch gone bad on January 28, 1986.

I remember that tragic event as if it were yesterday. It occurred a month to the day of our second daughter's birth. As a young pastor I was on my way to a church leadership retreat in the Santa Cruz Mountains of Northern California. Giant redwood trees scraping the sky punctuated the grounds of Mission Springs Conference Center where our retreat was held. Pointing heavenward these evergreen sentries stood at somber attention as our broken hearts knelt in corporate grief.

Later that day, President Reagan addressed a grieving nation as he eulogized the Challenger astronauts. Standing before television cameras, he borrowed lines from a famous poem that references the mystery of air travel and touching the face of God. It was a memorable quotation that captured the hearts of the American people.

Fast-forward ten years. Our family had moved from a suburb of San Francisco to the outskirts of Chicago where I had been called to a new parish. Annual visits to see my parents and my brother's family in

Wenatchee remained a priority. While vacationing in The Valley, I contacted friends from childhood. Those included Valerie Valaas, my high school French teacher. As one who celebrated my call to pastoral ministry following graduation, Madame Valaas asked if I had time to meet her priest at St. James Episcopal Church in Cashmere. She really liked him and thought I would enjoy visiting with him.

She was right. Pastor Hugh Magee was most gracious and kind. He expressed interest in my pastoral pursuits. He gave me a tour of the quaint sanctuary with stunning stained-glass windows. And then as we concluded our visit, Pastor Magee gave me an illuminated copy of a poem. He told me it was written by his brother. As I looked at the final lines of the verse, I recognized it the words President Reagan had quoted the day the Challenger had exploded. Amazingly, John Magee was Hugh's older brother.

Along with the beautifully designed rendering of High Flight, Pastor Magee gave me a copy of an article that chronicled the history of his brother and the poem. John Magee, like his brother Hugh, was a son of an American Episcopalian priest and his British wife who served as missionaries in China.

In 1941, as a nineteen-year-old, John would be awarded a scholarship to Yale University. Instead, he enlisted in the Royal Canadian Air Force where he became a pilot and was training to protect his mother's homeland from Hitler's advance. His love of flying is reflected in the words of his famous poem. Four months after penning High Flight, John was killed over England when his Spitfire aircraft accidentally collided with another plane.

Like the Challenger disaster, John Magee's untimely death will forever be associated with his words that continue to live on. If you have never read the entire poem, I commend it to you. As I understand it is included in most every memorial service for one who has served in the United States Air Force. Understandably, my copy of High Flight is a treasured poem. So is my memory of that unforgettable visit with the poet's brother who now is deceased.

A Godwink in the Garbage

Others might call it simply a coincidence, but I'd call it a Godwink.

The dumpster near to where I park my car at work was filled to the brim. I couldn't help noticing stacks of sheet music on top of a heap of plastic trash bags. I spent several minutes looking at an assortment of religious and secular music from the 40s and 50s. Having collected antique sheet music for years, I felt like I'd happened upon a gold mine.

And then I saw it! Sandwiched in-between a Bing Crosby hit and a Lawrence Welk score was a 1962 newspaper clipping from the Minneapolis Morning Tribune. I couldn't believe my eyes! The faded yellow article referenced a California youth leader by the name of Jack Hayford who had just won first place in a nationwide hymn-writing contest. The newspaper article also included the entire hymn (lyrics and music). It was a hymn I'd never heard of: "We Lift Our Voice Rejoicing."

But Jack Hayford was someone with whom I was very familiar. His worship chorus "Majesty," written in 1977 after traveling to England with his wife Anna during the silver jubilee of Queen Elizabeth's reign, has been a favorite of mine since I first heard it sung in my first pastorate. I loved how he compared the pomp and pageantry associated with the British royalty to the regal beauty and respect due the object of our worship each Sunday.

This eighty-eight-year-old retired pastor served The Church on the Way in Southern California for many years. He was the beloved minister to many a Hollywood celebrity. As a young pastor, I looked up to Jack Hayford as an example. He modeled for me how to use language with intentionality and bring God's Word to life poetically. His gift with language not only earned him a reputation as an eloquent preacher, he also wrote some six hundred hymns. It was Pastor Jack who inspired me to write lyrics to familiar hymn tunes for congregations I served.

Jack Hayford's brilliant mind and winsome personality brought respect and credibility to the Foursquare Gospel denomination that had been founded back in the 1920s by the controversial Aimee Semple McPherson. It was Jack Hayford who served as a mentor to young pastors like me and Doug Murren (with whom I went to Wenatchee High School in the Sixties) who became a leader in the Foursquare denomination.

But here's where the Godwink comes in. After rescuing the newspaper clipping from the garbage, I returned to my office to share my find with friends on Facebook. Only then did I learn that my pastoral hero had just died the day before. My discovery in the dumpster was a divine appointment of sorts. How else would a newspaper clipping from a newspaper publisher six decades before randomly have ended up in my hands the week of his death?

Although I never did meet Jack Hayford in person, twenty years ago I was tasked by a publisher to edit sermons by Pastor Jack for publication. The assignment also called for me to write chapter introductions that would precede each sermon in a book that came to be called "The Divine Visitor." And though Jack Hayford died on January 8, 2023, his ministry lives on with a prize volume on a shelf in my library.

Forget Looking for Shadows, Look in the Mirror

February is a month of special days. It's Black History Month. It's midwinter break month to get away for some skiing or sunshine. The midpoint of this 28-day month is Valentine's Day followed by Presidents Day. And, of course, it all kicks off with Groundhog Day.

I've never been to Gobbler's Knob in Punxsutawney, Pennsylvania on February 2nd, but I'm intrigued by the annual tradition that has put that small town on the map. The yearly pursuit of Punxsutawney Phil searching for his shadow has earned that cave-dwelling rodent celebrity status.

Thirty years ago *Groundhog Day*, starring Bill Murray and Andie McDowell, earned a place in popular culture. Ever since it's release, just the mention of Groundhog Day calls to mind the plight of being trapped in a 24-hour time loop.

Although the plot of that 1993 film is far-fetched, for those who have jobs that offer little variety or change of pace, life can seem like a perpetual Groundhog Day. But it's not just those who deal with repetitive job functions who feel their life journey is lived in cruise-control. If we are honest with ourselves, our day-in-and-day-out routines and rituals can render our daily lives devoid of a sense of adventure and creativity. While many find comfort in facing the familiar, most dream of doing something different.

This Groundhog Day, instead of being preoccupied with looking for shadows, why not focus on looking in the mirror? What do you like? What do you wish you could change? What will it take to bring about the change you desire? Chances are it will require rebooting one's routine.

I can't remember where I first heard it, but I've never forgotten it. *Insanity is doing the same thing over and over again and expecting different results.*

It's true! And yet we are guilty of acting insane a lot of the time. We fall into mindless behavior patterns without thinking about the consequences for others or to ourselves.

But looking into the mirror instead of looking for shadows is only the first step. Once you take a good hard look at what you see, you will need to decide what to do with what seems out of place. It will require acting on what you've discovered.

There's a memorable verse in the New Testament that underscores the importance of following through on what we understand needs to change. The Epistle of James chides the first-century faithful to not simply give mental assent to something they claim to believe, but to actually put feet to their faith.

"Do not merely listen to the word, and so deceive yourselves. Do what it says. Anyone who listens to the word but does not do what it says is like someone who looks at his face in a mirror and, after looking at himself, goes away and immediately forgets what he looks like." (James 1:22-24)

A month into this new year, some resolutions have already been coded and carried to the morgue. But it's not too late to establish some new action steps to make the most out of 2023.

We still have time to breathe new life into our diets, revisit our fitness routine, revive our spiritual disciplines, alter our schedule with family, renew our volunteer commitments and establish sacred times to take care of ourselves.

Speaking of shadows, there is one shadow I would suggest looking for and attempting to follow. As I person of the cloth, throughout my life

I've attempted to take my cues from a first century rabbi who began his career as a carpenter.

Jesus of Nazareth offers me a great example of one who cared for others and himself while refusing to be defined by inflexible routines. Maybe following his shadow would be a worthy pursuit for you as well. Not just on Groundhog Day, but every day.

A Celebration of a Fifty Year Friendship

K-J-R Seattle, channel 95. I loved that jingle on my favorite radio station. As a Pentecostal preacher's kid in the early sixties, I wasn't allowed to go to movies or dances. But my parents did allow me to listen to top 40 radio. I loved hearing Pat O'Day's unique voice. His signature cadence and the way he modulated his voice set him apart from his peers. While I first heard the Beatles on the Ed Sullivan Show when I was in a sixth grader, it was KJR to which I tuned to hear the Fab Four's hits on a daily basis.

By the time I went to college in the fall of 1970, I was a loyal KJR listener. I would do my homework in my dorm room at Seattle Pacific with the radio on in the background. The likes of Norm Gregory, Bobby Simon, Gary Shannon, Tom Murphy and Emperor Smith helped me make it through a challenging freshman year.

One afternoon in the spring of 1971, I was listening to 'JR while typing a term paper. I heard a voice I didn't recognize. The deejay identified himself as Tom Murphy's replacement for the day. It was George Toles. I was impressed by this new guy's wordsmithing ability while introducing a new single. As a Christian, I was sensitive to his subtle nuancing of song intros that bespoke his own faith. From time to time that spring, I heard George filling in for other regular deejays. He quickly became my favorite jock.

Fast-forward to the summer of 1971. I was back home in Wenatchee working my part-time job at a local radio station. The station manager had given me a three-hour shift that I could program myself. Even though KUEN was primarily a country station, I was permitted to play top 40 singles and add my own patter in between records.

On a Friday evening in July, I was at the radio station in the control room spinning records. Because it was after hours, the front door to the station was locked. But since the control room faced the street, I could see someone was at the door. When I went to see what the stranger wanted, I was met with a warm smile and friendly greeting. "My name is George Toles. My wife and I heard your program while driving over Blewitt Pass. I just wanted to stop by and let you know you're doing a fine job."

I was speechless. George Toles? Really? At my little rinky dink radio station? He had heard me on-air? He thought I was good? I couldn't believe it. Obviously, I welcomed him in and told him that I knew who he was. I referenced my appreciation for his work at KJR. Somehow, we recognized that we were both followers of Jesus. George said he and his wife Liz were in town for the weekend. He asked if I could meet them for breakfast the next morning. I willingly accepted his invitation. After breakfast I had to go to my other part-time job as a salesman at the local men's store in town. George and Liz stopped by The Varsity Line later in the day because he claimed to need a new pair of socks. Hmmm. Whether he did or not remains a mystery. My guess is that he simply wanted to stop and see where I worked and sock-it to me with more encouragement.

As they say, the rest is history. That random meeting forty-nine years ago resulted in a close-knit friendship that continues to this day. As a college kid, George would offer me a pass to Sonics games from time to time. He turned me on to Christian rock and roll during the Jesus People Movement. He introduced me to Frank Thompson, the news director at KJR who in turn helped me process my career goals.

George became a mentor of sorts as I pursued pastoral ministry while always keeping a finger in broadcasting. After I married and my wife and I moved to California and then to Illinois and then back to Washington, the ties remained tight. George has always been there at strategic crossroads in my life. He was a key encourager when I battled a season of clinical depression. He counseled me when I faced criticism from difficult congregants. He helped me think out-of-the-box when tired routines begged for a fresh vision.

I owe more to George Toles than I can possibly express. Through the years I have benefited from this colleague in ministry who was the older brother I never had. I have a manila file filled with personal handwritten notes George sent to me just at the right time. And each one is signed with his signature sign-off, "In His Grip!" Even though we saw each other more when I was living in Chicagoland (where he would visit his wife's family twice a year) than we do since I moved back to Seattle in 2005, George Toles remains a significant part of my life.

His ministry through His Deal (formerly known as Nordy's) is a motivating metaphor. It pictures how effective ministry can continue even when complicated by less-than-ideal health. In George I see a modern-day Apostle Paul. Like that first century Bible author, George battles a thorn in the flesh while finding God's grace sufficient. And I for one am grateful.

They Had a Dream! What's Yours?

This month our nation pauses to look up to a man who was looked down on for the majority of his brief life. Martin Luther King, Jr. was only five feet six inches tall. But his stature as a civil rights activist still renders him a giant fifty-five years after his death at the age of thirty-nine.

This year marks the sixtieth anniversary of the dream Dr. King so eloquently articulated on the steps of the Lincoln Memorial to a crowd of some 250,000 people. Many of us can recite portions of that famous speech that pictured a future day when the content of a person's character matters more than the color of their skin.

How could we have known that less than three months after Dr. King voiced his vision our beloved President would be gunned down in Dallas by the hate that violently stalked our country? All the same, Dr. King's dream was swallowed up by a national nightmare.

Well, that was 1963. A century earlier in 1861 another member of a minority group verbalized a dream for our country. It was a dream that was cast against the backdrop of racial strife and a bloody civil war. Her name was Julia Ward Howe.

After visiting President Lincoln in the White House, this abolitionist and women's rights activist put pen to paper. Her vision for a deeply divided country was captured in a poetic expression that portrayed a preferred future. The republic she envisioned would benefit from a focused understanding of the past as well as from looking forward to what might yet be.

Mrs. Howe's eyes saw the glory of the coming of the Lord where the values of God's Kingdom would become the values of America. She set her lyrics to a well-known military tune (John Brown's Body). Less than a year later (in February 1862), "The Battle Hymn of the Republic" would be published for the first time in the Atlantic Monthly.

Although these two visions for America were separated by more than a hundred years, both Dr. King's dream and Julia Ward Howe's dream share something in common. Both dreams were conceived and birthed in the Willard Hotel just a couple blocks from the White House. Isn't that amazing? That historic structure on Pennsylvania Avenue, where Presidents, international statesmen and entertainers have stayed, is a tangible reminder of dreams yet to be fully realized.

Racial injustice, political division, religious persecution, gun violence and spiritual apathy continue to pollute our national landscape. They, among other things, are to blame for dreams remaining dreams instead of becoming a reality. The words of both dreamers are needed now more than ever. But they are not the only words that are needed.

While Dr. King's dream and Mrs. Howe's vision for America are well-known, they are not the only pictures of a preferred future worth framing. I have a dream for what our nation should look like. I'm guessing you do, too.

Our dreams may never be set to music or be engraved in limestone in the Washington D.C., but they are worthy of being written down. They are worthy of being shared and discussed within our spheres of influence.

This year, instead of coming up with personal resolutions for a new year, why not try your hand a documenting your dream for America? Or how about an acrostic that conveys what our nation needs to thrive?

Here's mine: **A**merica **M**ust **E**mbrace **R**ighteousness, **I**ntegrity, **C**ompassion and **A**ccountability. What's yours?

We Don't Talk About...

Last summer my five-year-old and three-year-old granddaughters were watching the Disney movie *Encanto* repeatedly. As a result, long after the show was over, they were still singing the lyrics to the music. One of their favorite songs was *"We Don't Talk About Bruno."*

If you've seen the Disney animated feature-length film, you know why the Family Madrigal didn't speak about a brother who had fallen out of favor with his siblings. In all likelihood there is a Bruno in your extended family who you rarely talk about (or talk to) because of issues that remain unresolved. Branches of a family tree that are no longer attached to the limbs that nourished their growth and development are all-too common.

As a chaplain in a retirement community, I officiate at more than a few funerals and memorial services annually. On our campus we lose about ten percent of our residents each year who leave us through the doorway of death. Most of these bittersweet celebrations of life fill my heart with gratitude and joy. It is very meaningful to witness family members publicly paying homage to their spouses, grandparents, parents or siblings.

But I must confess there are far too many occasions where estrangement within a family finds adult siblings sitting at memorial service on opposite sides of the church. These family members avoid each other and refuse to speak. Once, when I was a pastor, one of the adult children chose not to attend his mother's memorial even though his father was expecting him to sit beside him. The program indicated that he would be one of the speakers. As it turned out, the son didn't want to be in proximity of his sister and so chose to stay at home. It broke my heart.

However, it's not just at a parent's funeral when broken relationships within a clan are most apparent. Empty places at the family dinner table over Christmas and Hannukah leave a bitter taste that can't be ameliorated by simply passing the sugar bowl. Weddings, baptisms, bar mitzvas, birthday parties and anniversary celebrations are occasions when those "missing in action" rob the room of potential joy.

And it may not be a family member at all. Perhaps the person you intentionally refuse to talk about or include in your social life is a colleague at work or a neighbor. Once you considered them a friend or a trusted ally, but no longer. The fact that alienation exists suggests that either that person or you are aliens to one another.

At the start of this new year, we are given an opportunity to do more than make resolutions. We can actually make reparations. We can take steps toward repairing what has been broken.

A new year for me means a new day planner. Even though much of what I do at work is chronicled through Outlook on my smart phone and laptop, I am still part of a generation that relies on a paper calendar. And the acquisition of my new planner provides me with a tangible joy I can't quite explain.

That blank calendar like the new year signifies new beginnings. It is unblemished and unstained. Blank squares invite new appointments and commitments. That new calendar, as well as this new year, provides new opportunities to revisit old wounds and to consider new ways of treating those wounds. A new year invites us to take baby steps toward the realization of a dream in which estranged family members or friends walk back into our lives.

In the case of Bruno, the estranged brother in *Encanto*, responsibility for alienation was owned by the appropriate parties. Forgiveness was offered. Relationship was restored. A branch was restored to the limb to which it belonged. But that's Hollywood.

When it comes to the Brunos in our lives, there's no guarantee that reconciliation will occur. But then again, there's no hope without trying. Here's to hoping!

A Classic Movie with Timeless Message

Last month was Breast Cancer Awareness month. But for the last twenty-five years or so, October has also been observed as Pastor Appreciation Month. Churches throughout the country look for tangible ways to recognize pastors and priests for the contribution they make in our lives.

Needless-to-say, clergy serve on the frontlines of warring factors in our culture. They play a significant role in combatting injustice and self-destructive tendencies. Often, however, their efforts are overlooked. Their attempts at compassion are easily camouflaged. At the retirement community where I serve as chaplain, we recently invited area clergy to our campus and honored them with a special lunch and a small gift. They were grateful.

Having been in the ministry for more than four decades, I know firsthand the joys and challenges pastors face week in and week out year after year. Someone has aptly stated that the clergy person's rewards are out of this world. But the struggles he or she faces are very much in the here-and-now.

One of those challenges common to the typical clergyman is taming the inner beast known as ego. What pastor or priest has not wanted to grow his congregation or parish? What person of the cloth has not looked for tangible ways to earn the respect and recognition of his or her peers? Who of them has not known the hunger for power and influence that becomes insatiable at times?

While that unhealthy hunger is hardly abnormal, it is also hardly new. The lust for power and recognition has cost too many celebrity pastors their reputation. The inner conflict that can destroy the gifted has been dramatized on the silver screen over the decades.

One of those films celebrates its 75th anniversary this year. "The Bishop's Wife" starring David Niven, Loretta Young and Cary Grant portrays the inner struggle of an ambition-driven cleric. Although this timeless picture was remade in 1996 as "The Preacher's Wife" (with Whitney Houston and Denzel Washington), there is no replacing the original. I ought to know. "The Bishop's Wife" is this chaplain's wife's favorite Christmas film. We watch it every year.

One of the actors in "The Bishop's Wife" is a friend of mine. Karolyn Grimes, who played the part of Debby (the Bishop's young daughter) is now eighty-two years old. Karolyn was also in "It's a Wonderful Life" (my favorite Christmas movie) as George Bailey's daughter Zuzu. Having spent time with Karolyn, I know that playing the role of the bishop's daughter was a highlight of her young acting career.

Curiously, Karolyn once told me that David Niven (who portrayed the ego-motivated minister in "The Bishop's Wife") had his own struggles as an actor. He didn't like children. Karolyn related much better to Cary Grant, whose angelic role on screen was replicated in real life.

As with Frank Capra's "Wonderful" film about Mary Bailey's husband George, "The Bishop's Wife" deals with a dark plot. In both black-and-white classics, we see desperate men calling on God for guidance. In the underrated movie that exposes the over-ambitious clergyman, the film ends with a redemptive conclusion. The bishop discovers his identity is not tied to the construction of a new cathedral. Instead, he finds (with the help of an angel) that his life and ministry is most fulfilled by serving those most in need of his care. And those include his wife and daughter.

As one who has tasted the sweet (but forbidden) fruit of ambition, I understand the seductive nature of success. A bout with clinical depression thirty years ago proved to be the reality check I needed. An undisciplined ego demands a high cost. Examining my motives, I determined to invest my limited energy in those around me. As a result, this chaplain's wife can attest to my contentment and hers.

And so I commend to you "The Bishop's Wife." This movie celebrating a milestone anniversary offers a glimpse of the humanity of those clothed in holy garb. But it also reminds us that investing in people (and not brick-and-mortar) results in the most lasting value.

In Search of Balance

Earlier this fall I was attending a leadership summit in a suburb of Chicago. Following our sessions one afternoon, I went for a power walk before dinner. Adjacent to the conference center was a cemetery. Because reading old headstones in a graveyard is one of my favorite pastimes, my aspirations of getting my heartrate up gave in to my curiosity as I looked down at the markers.

One tombstone in particular captured my attention. It marked the final resting place for a family by the name of Balance. Balance? Really? I'd never seen that word as a name before. For one whose mind delights in word play and double entendres, I had to smile. Balance was dead.

Before me was living proof that balance had been a casualty of life. What was relationally true for this Chicago-area family, has been emotionally true for me at times in the past when my schedule was out of control. And I know I'm not alone. Balance is that easy-going, less-than-obvious, reality that doesn't call attention to itself. We tend to take it for granted. We don't realize how key it is to a happy life until it's gone.

When balance bites the dust, panic thrives. Life becomes chaotic. A kind of grief sets in. Inner peace plays hide-and-seek. When balance has ceased to be a reality in our lives, the consequences are endless. They include debt, illness, depression, a short temper, drug use, alcohol abuse and over-eating.

If ever there is a time when taking urgent care of balance is critical, it's now. This is the season of the year when maintaining a healthy balance between demands and desires is at-risk. Advent, Hanukkah and Christmas can easily find balance on life-support.

Just looking at my own schedule at work is enough to rob balance of its breath. There is a tree-lighting ceremony, a St. Lucia breakfast, a poetry reading tea, four holiday concerts, three Advent lectures, two staff parties and an all-campus carol sing-a-long. (Were you expecting a partridge in a pear tree?)

And then there's my own personal calendar of writing the family Christmas letter, addressing the Christmas cards, shopping for family members and workmates, wrapping those gifts and helping my wife decorate the house.

Add to all of the above the fact that Christmas Day falls on Sunday this year. Bah! Humbug! Once again, a day meant to be spent with family is threatened by the demands of the church calendar. Without an infusion of creativity, balance is definitely headed for the intensive care unit.

Your schedule is likely just as complicated. The commitments on your calendar may be different than mine, but the outcome is equally as stressful. With apologies to Dr. Seuss, it's not the Grinch we have to worry about. It's the lack of balance that threatens to steal Christmas (and ultimately our health).

To that end may I suggest reflecting on the lyrics of one of my most-loved contemporary carols. In "Breath of Heaven" (written by Chris Eaton and recorded by Amy Grant) there is recognition of the weight waiting for Christmas finds us carrying as well as the pressures that cause us to stoop navigating life in a less-than-perfect world.

I am waiting in a silent prayer. I am frightened by the load I bear, In a world as cold as stone. Must I walk this path alone? Be with me now.

In silent prayer and honest reflection, we just might find guidance in how to reduce the activities that typically define our December. We just might discover that Immanuel (God-with-us) is with us providing us the means to keep balance alive.

In the case of Christmas Day being on Sunday, for me there is hope. Balance will not succumb this year to the life-threatening complications with which I have to contend every six years. With the concurrence of colleagues, we decided to pre-record our Christmas Day worship service and broadcast it on our closed-circuit television channel a few times on Sunday. A hack we discovered during COVID proves helpful once again.

Now, what other ways can I simplify this season?

Picturing Contentment: Life Lessons from the Original Facebook

The other day I came across my student pictorial directory from Fuller Seminary. Of course, I looked for the page where my face was pictured. I was amazed at how much I've aged in 45 years. The fact is this. Inside I feel I'm still that twenty-five-year-old pastor-in-training. I'm guessing you know what I mean. In spite of the number of candles on our birthday cake, the person inside the one who blows remains the same age.

As I thumbed through the directory, I made note of classmates who walked the same halls and ate in the same dining room as I did. I saw Gary Walter, who would eventually be elected president of a major Protestant denomination. And then there was Mark Galli, a Masters of Divinity student like me, who would become editor-in-chief of Christianity Today, the preeminent go-to periodical for North American pastors.

I saw a photo of Robert A. Schuller (son of the famed Crystal Cathedral pastor) who would take over the ministry of his famous father. There was Bruce Narramore who, with his uncle, would start the Rosemead School of Psychology.

As I kept turning the dogeared pages, I saw Neil Clark Warren. This psychology professor would find his niche several years later as the founder of eHarmony (one of the first online dating services). And then there was a mug-like photo of a very young Michael Youssef who would go on to become an internationally-known televangelist based in Atlanta.

Page after page revealed photos of classmates who would go on to distinguish themselves as Christian musicians, mega-church pastors, college professors, best-selling authors, advertising executives and book publishers. As I realized the success so many of my former classmates had experienced, I felt a twinge of envy. What might I have done differently that would have resulted in a more influential trajectory? What did I opt for as a student that limited my potential as a pastor? Should I have spent more time with the books than exploring Southern California on weekends?

But my mental dance with the green-eyed monster began to slow to a stop. I looked up from the pictures in the directory and started looking back over my life. I made note of at the unique opportunities I've had since 1977. No, my resume doesn't even begin to compare with a Robert Schuller or a Mark Galli or a Michael Youssef. But the people I've met, the churches I've served, the places to which I've traveled and the experiences I've been afforded have resulted in more blessings than I deserve.

Walking the halls of my memory and looking up at the portraits on the wall (actually on the pages of my directory) resulted in an overwhelming sense of gratitude. Embracing the opportunities and experiences God allows us is the first step in learning the dance steps of contentment.

Like George Bailey (in my favorite Christmas movie) who never experienced the wealth or success of his high school classmate Sam Wainwright, I relate to someone who has not known the outcomes of his childhood dreams. But when all is said and done, I've had a pretty wonderful life after all. I'm guessing you have had a wonderful life as well.

There Actually is Crying in Baseball!

There's a line in the movie *A League of Their Own* where Tom Hanks' character says, *"There's no crying in baseball!"* And while I love that film almost as much as I do *Field of Dreams*, I take exception with the quote about crying.

When it came to baseball, I cried a lot as a kid. Sixty-one years ago, I was a nine-year-old following Mickey Mantle's attempt to break Babe Ruth's home run record. "The Mick" was my hero. My mom made me a Yankees jersey complete with and Mantle's number 7 on the back. I was crestfallen when Roger Maris hit sixty-one homers.

The next year I cried myself to sleep listening to the Seattle Rainiers on my transistor radio. The minor league farm team of the Boston Red Sox stole my heart and then proceed to break it.

Whereas they had taken first place the previous season, the 1962 Rainiers finished in fourth place fifteen games behind San Diego. The mesmerizing voices of play-by-play announcers Keith Jackson and Lee Desilet pictured for me the lackluster performances of my favorite players on the diamond. Could my team ever repeat as champions? I wondered. I hoped. I cried.

Fast-forward a half-dozen years. Seattle gets a major league baseball team. But the Pilots taxi for an entire season and never really take off. The team leaves town. More reason for sadness.

A decade later a team called the Mainers docks in Seattle. And baseball fans flock to the Kingdome with hopes the Mariners will prove once and for all that Seattle truly is a baseball town. And the fan loyalty shown the Ms made such a case. But, with the exception of a couple of seasons in which the Mariners made an impressive run for the Fall Classic, drought-weary fans have had reason to cry. We are the only team never to have played in the World Series. And what is worse, we haven't made the playoffs in two decades.

But, alas, this year our tears of sorrow have been replaced by tears of joy. For the first time since 2001, we are playing games beyond the regular season. A never-ending-season of sadness has given way to a season of joy. Regardless, of how far our team advances in the playoffs, we have reason to kick up our heels.

To celebrate our team's amazing accomplishments this year, I was asked to display my extensive Mariners memorabilia at Covenant Living at the Shores. Forty-five years of waiting for a World Series appearance has resulted in quite a collection of which my colleagues aware.

When I learned that a couple on our campus still have their Kingdome program from the very first Mariners' home game in 1977, I asked if they'd be willing to add it to my display. Denny and Sharron Horn enthusiastically agreed. The wait for something to celebrate has been equally as long for them.

There is a verse in the Bible that puts into context the times in our lives when we find ourselves waiting for hoped-for happiness. In Psalm 30 the writer observes, *"Weeping may last for the night, but joy comes in the morning."* In other words, times of sorrow eventually give way to times of rejoicing.

If you grew up cheering for the Chicago Cubs, you know how very long that night of weeping can be. But the truth of that passage has to do with much more than heartache related to the hometown team. It has to do with grief at home when a family member loses their extra-inning battle with cancer. It has to do with the tears that come with unexpected unemployment or an undesired divorce. Yes, there *is* crying in baseball as well as in life.

And it's true. Waiting for a good outcome can be long and painful. But the promise of the passage in Psalms offers reason to hold out for a positive result. I love the way the psalm concludes. *"You turned my wailing into dancing; you removed my sackcloth and clothed me with joy..."*

The Hunger in My Heart

It was the summer of 1960. It was a summer I will never forget.

I had just completed second grade. My maternal grandfather, an immigrant from Norway, turning seventy-five. To celebrate this milestone, Papa Birkeland was taking my Nana and their three adult children and spouses to Norway.

In addition to spending time with Norwegian relatives in the small town where my grandfather was born, they would explore Europe. My mom and dad would stay on to visit the village where my paternal grandfather was raised in Greece.

It was the opportunity of a lifetime. It was a trip that would last six weeks. It would be the longest time my six-year-old brother and I would have been separated from our parents.

Even though my dad had only been pastor of his church for three years, the leadership was willing to give him an early sabbatical. I was less willing to have my parents leave.

Arrangements were made with a widow in our congregation who would stay in our home. Mrs. Costello was a retired kindergarten teacher who had a knack with young children. My mom helped ease the anticipated separation anxiety by wrapping small gifts that my brother and I would open each day.

A few days after the tearful farewell, the unexpected occurred. Mrs. Costello took ill. She explained her predicament to a family in the church who cared for foster kids. The Jubbs agreed to take us in.

Initially our new "home" seemed exciting. There were a multitude of dogs, a strawberry patch from which to pick and six kids with whom to play. But when it came time for bath night on Saturdays, the same water was used for each child. By the time my turn came, I remember the water being less than transparent and not very hot.

My parents wrote letters from their various destinations that were forwarded to the Jubbs' home. As a soon-to-be third grader, I read the correspondence to my little brother while we both fought back tears.

Sundays found us being chauffeured to church in the Jubbs' station wagon. Because they were not all that connected to the church, they only stayed for Sunday school. As families were filing into the sanctuary for worship, Marc and I found our place in the way-back of the wood paneled Chevy.

For the first three Sundays, getting to skip church (something this pastor's kid had never experienced before) was kinda fun. Going to Sunday school and then having more time to play was a novelty. But come the fourth Sunday, my mood began to change.

I not only was missing my mom and dad, I was missing the routine of worship. Three weeks without singing the hymns or hearing a sermon left me hungering for what was so much a part of my Sunday routine. Not seeing the familiar faces of those who comprised the core of the congregation intensified my feelings of loneliness. Even at eight years of age, I realized how much the morning worship service meant to me.

On that fourth Sunday as the Jubbs were making their predictable getaway, I made my escape. Finding my way into the sanctuary, I snagged a seat on the aisle hoping not to be spotted.

I noticed the white linen cloth covering the communion table. An inner warmth washed over me. Today was Communion Sunday. That solemn ceremony at the end of the service was something I looked forward to each month. It helped me visualize how much God loved me. Again it occurred to me that I was homesick for more than my mom and dad, I was missing my church family.

As I sat down following the singing of the opening hymn, I felt a hand on my shoulder. I turned to see an usher motioning me to follow him. My attempted escape had been discovered. My plan had been foiled.

For the next two weeks, until my parents returned from their European adventure, I was forced to fit into the worship-less practice of my temporary family. It revealed to me the importance of worship I still affirm more than sixty years later.

An Invitation to Paint Rocks

During the height of COVID, quarantined artists in my community found creative expression for their talent. They painted rocks and left them camouflaged on the nature trail where my wife and I walk several days a week. Happening upon them was like finding hidden Easter eggs. The messages and images on the brightly colored stones were uplifting. They reminded us to mask up and reach out to one another (all the while maintaining social distance).

A few months ago I discovered a painted stone perched near a tree on our trail. At first glance it reminded me of a multi-colored oblong-shaped Rubik's cube. But upon closer examination, I realized it was a rock with the colors of the Ukrainian flag and a red heart. The realization prompted a holy moment of introspection.

That unnamed artist unexpectedly and unknowingly challenged me to live out the values we celebrated just a month ago while grilling burgers and watching fireworks. That brightly colored stone reminded me that freedom can't be taken for granted. It must be defended and preserved at all cost.

With a stroke of a paintbrush, the rock painter demonstrated love for people we have never met who are defending their homeland all the while fighting for the freedoms we take for granted. That painted rock was a sermon of sorts. Its message found its mark.

Similar sermons are being "preached" all around us. It warms my heart to see my neighbors flying Ukrainian flags. Similarly, we see messages on social media continually calling us to support Ukraine. Residents at the retirement home where I work have created Ukrainian flags out of light blue and bright yellow construction paper. They display these makeshift banners in their windows. In our Sunday worship services, we pray for President Zelenskyy and the innocent victims of Putin's war.

Decades ago Edgar Guest (known as the people's poet) wrote one of his more memorable rhymes called *Sermons We See*. In it he mused about how belief is best communicated. As a pastor and as a poet, I am inspired by Guest's words and his example.

I'd rather see a sermon than hear one any day;
I'd rather one should walk with me than merely tell the way.
The eye's a better pupil and more willing than the ear,
Fine counsel is confusing, but example's always clear;
And the best of all the preachers are the men who live their creeds,
For to see good put in action is what everybody needs.

Flying a flag. Painting a rock. Writing a letter to a Congressman. Contributing to organizations that sponsor displaced refugees. Praying for God to change the heart of a war-mongering Russian president. All these are ways to dress our values in work clothes and put feet to our faith.

A first-century follower of Jesus "painted a rock" by writing a letter. His name was James. Against a backdrop of Christians whose faith was ethereal and philosophical, James swam upstream against the tide of popular option. What he scrawled on a scroll of parchment promoted the concept of "practicing what we preach." Saint James wrote, *someone will say, "You have faith; I have deeds." Show me your faith without deeds, and I will show you my faith by my deeds.*

Another well-known Saint by the name of Francis is credited with having said, *"Preach the Gospel at all times. If necessary, use words."* Based on the research I have done, St. Francis didn't actually say those words. But his life of action and reaction underscores their truth. Validating our values with good works is essential. So, how about it? Let's start "painting rocks."

Skookum, Santa and the Searching Eyes of God

Our family moved to Wenatchee fifty-eight years ago this week. An iconic sign with moveable eyes welcomed us as we entered town. The Skookum Indian greeted us with a knowing gaze. As a twelve-year-old I was impressed by the searching eyes and the eventual wink of that motorized apple label image.

Although I moved away from the valley when I graduated from college, regular visits home to see my parents and my brother weren't complete with exchanging glances with Skookum. After I married, family vacations inevitably included trips to Wenatchee for my three daughters to be spoiled by their grandparents.

As we drove into town, I would alert my girls to the fact that Skookum was looking for them. With excitement Kristin, Allison and Lauren would crane their necks to look for the searching eyes of that friendly face. When one of the those moving eyes winked, they laughed with glee. They were convinced that the young Indian brave had spotted them.

Although that familiar image no longer graces the skyline of our town, I picture Skookum each time I drive the Avenue. For me, that face was a tangible reminder that my Father in Heaven is continually aware of what is going on in my life. And that's a comforting thought.

At Christmastime we refer to the omniscience of Santa while singing *"He sees you when you're sleeping. He knows when you're awake. He knows if you've been bad or good so be good for goodness' sake..."* The lyrics of that holiday classic are meant to motivate little ones to be on their best behavior throughout the year.

Looking back, however, my sense is that the never-sleeping eyes of Santa are viewed through the lens of guilt or threat. *"You'd better watch out! I'm telling you why…"*

The supernatural traits ascribed to that fictional Yuletide figure actually derive from One who truly is all-knowing and ever-present. The God we worship, as the old African American spiritual declares, *"never sleeps. He never slumbers. He watches over you both night and day…"*

Whereas some view that cosmic all-seeing eye with a sense of dread, I find a sense of comfort in knowing that nothing escapes the purview of Providence. There is a passage in the Old Testament that references the searching eyes of God. It's found in 2 Chronicles 16:9. *"The eyes of the LORD search the whole earth in order to strengthen those whose hearts are fully committed to him."*

Rather than thinking of God's awareness of our attitudes, actions and reactions from a negative point of view, the aforementioned Scripture suggests that God's focus on our lives is a good thing. It is intended to have beneficial results. In other words, God's awareness of my desire to please Him has a promised payoff.

The all-knowing nature of God is nothing to be feared. It is a truth to take hold of with gratitude. When we feel like nobody knows the trouble we've seen, we can be assured of the fact that God knows and cares.

Several years ago our family was traveling in Greece visiting the village from which my paternal grandfather immigrated to America. My girls, now grown, were introduced to an icon of an eye sold by a street vendor. This blue and white glass ornament symbolized the eye of God. This beautiful keepsake conveyed a simple but profound truth.

Unlike the winking eye of a Wenatchee icon that had defined their childhood, this "God's eye" didn't wink. It is a constant reminder, to my children and to me, of God's continual awareness and His constant care. I, for one, am glad He never sleeps.

No Vacation from Vocation

This is the weekend that marks the unofficial end of summer. In reality, we have three more weeks until the autumnal equinox. But with school back in session and the days growing shorter, it definitely does feel like summer has kissed us goodbye.

But summer's final kiss comes with an opportunity to kick-up our heels and let our hair down for a few days away from jobs and the daily routines that tax our emotions and drain our energy. Such a mini-vacation is a welcomed relief even though it might come with all the jobs related to closing up the vacation cottage for the season. Even with rest and relaxation, there are tasks that need to be done.

Our tradition for Labor Day finds us gathering the family at Lake Chelan. Our annual get together includes breakfasts on the deck, morning walks, kayaking, paddleboarding, grilling out, an 8-ball tournament, corn hole competition and golf. The fact that my two sons-in-law are lovers of the links demands that golf be part of this end-of-summer getaway. A trophy has even been purchased to crown this year's champion.

While Labor Day is a three-day-weekend from our jobs, a vocation is not something you can escape. Let me try to explain. A vocation is more than the work we do forty hours-a-week. If you Google the word *vocation* you'll discover that it comes from a Latin root meaning to call. Our vocation is our calling in life and that may or may not be synonymous with the job we have. In all likelihood, it is what we enjoy doing and make time to do whether we get paid for doing it or not.

All the same, there is confusion when comparing our occupations to a calling. Pastors often say they were "called" to the ministry. And what they do on Sundays (and every day in-between) is in fact their sacred vocation. And pastors are always "on call." But outside of the clergy, I'm not familiar with many who refer to what they do in terms of a sense of call.

Still most people I know confuse the word vocation with their employment. If someone were to ask you what your vocation is, it is quite likely you would respond with what you do for a living. But a better answer would be what it is that you feel passionate about doing with your life. What investment of your time brings you the most joy? Is it creating art? Is it taking photos? Is it writing music? Or performing music? Is it teaching young people? Is it serving older folks? Perhaps it's visiting patients in the hospital. Or maybe it's guiding hikers on trails through the Pacific Northwest wilderness. Or perhaps it's going on hikes yourself.

Your vocation is most likely what you do in your free time after you've put in your forty-hours on the job. One's occupation is what occupies your day in exchange for a paycheck. But a vocation is much more than occupying time. It is akin to what occupies your heart. If a vocation is a calling, it quite likely is what you hear your heart calling you to do. And all the better if you can earn your living doing that very thing.

I really like the way the late Frederick Buechner described finding yourself at the intersection of passion and plight. He said, *"The place God calls you to is the place where your deep gladness and the world's deep hunger meet."* How wonderful it is when what our heart calls us to do makes a practical difference in meeting a practical human need.

So for the next couple days, why not spend a portion of your vacation from your job contemplating how you increasingly invest your free time making the world a better place by doing what you love? Labor Day Weekend may be a break from your job, but it's not a vacation from your vocation.

A Labor Day Weekend Reflection

Having just retired in June, I approach this Labor Day with mixed emotions. I'm very grateful for a day to spend at Lake Chelan with the family enjoying annual traditions that define this unofficial end-of-summer holiday. All the same, a day that celebrates the gift of employment now finds me unemployed. And in all honesty, I am feeling a bit at sixes-and-sevens.

I've been a man-of-the-cloth for forty-five years. As such I had a flock to lead, a parish in which to preach, babies to baptize and couples to counsel. Clothed in the vestments of my calling, I knew what to do. With daily commitments to which to give myself, I felt dressed-for-success.

But now, without a job, I feel naked. There are no sermons to prepare, no shut-ins to visit, no grief support groups to facilitate. My calendar is uncharacteristically clear. The unblemished boxes on my Daytimer is a bit unsettling. As a result, I am laboring to make peace with my present status. Looking into the morning mirror I realize how much I have allowed my identity to be tied the title on my business card.

Although I have been quick to advise others to not equate their worth to their work, I find myself struggling to practice what I have preached. Now that I'm retired, I realize how easy it is to worship what we do. In the process, we fail to see our careers as simply a means to an end and blindly view them as the ultimate aim of our lives.

Gordon Dahl, a professor in the economist department at the University of California at San Diego, has indicated that we Americans tend to *worship our work, work at our play and play at our worship*. Having been guilty of giving my job unjustified adoration, I concur with his assessment. From what I've observed, we tend to be more fixated on what we do than focus on who we are. As you have no doubt heard before, we are humans doing instead of humans being.

A first century rabbi writing to a congregation in the Middle East offers a corrective to our tendency to elevate our employment. Paul of Tarsus wrote, "For we are God's workmanship, created to do good works, which God prepared in advance as our way of life." Notice the reference to workmanship and work.

As I reflect on that ancient rabbi's observation, it occurs to me that the labor worth celebrating this Labor Day is not our work in the office but God's work in our lives. Indeed, our worth as individuals has little to do with the job title on a name plate or the dollar amount on a W-2 form. Our worth is based in the fact that we are created in the image of our Creator. *Imago Dei* is the value with which each of us is tagged as we find ourselves at the starting line in the human race. In other words, we are the priceless product of God's efforts apart from our efforts.

But in addition to God's working within us, there is work for us to do tied to our God-likeness that gives meaning to our lives. The rabbi's words also call attention to the fact that the work that most matters is not a merely a 9-to-5 assignment for which we get paid. Rather, it involves investing in people through acts of kindness. This Labor Day why not join me in identifying work to which we can give ourselves apart from our employment status? Such efforts might include: visiting someone on hospice, mowing the lawn of a widow, volunteering as a greeter at church, giving your air miles to a young family planning a vacation, helping cook a meal in a homeless shelter, writing a letter of gratitude to a teacher you had in high school and giving a server in a favorite café an over-the-top tip.

Let's make this Labor Day not about our work but about other's worth. In the process we just might rediscover what our true work in this world is all about (whether we collect a paycheck or Social Security).

Let's Hear it for Family Reunions

Following our daughter's wedding, my wife and I hosted a family reunion. Because Wendy's siblings and their mates had come from Florida, Virginia and California, we wanted to spend additional time with them. The last time we were together was three years ago to celebrate my in-laws' 90th birthdays and 70th wedding anniversary.

Although I attended reunions of extended family members when I was a kid, my fascination with family reunions has grown since I've had children of my own. In the summer of 2001, my wife's parents gathered the children, spouses and grandchildren to celebrate their 50th anniversary. They chose Seaside, Oregon because it was where Hugh and Norma had honeymooned. The week we spent together was wonderful. A reporter from the local newspaper did a feature article on "the honeymooners" who had returned to celebrate their union fifty years later.

In addition to sharing memories of years past, we made new memories doing fun things. It was such a meaningful time we decided to try to have a reunion every five years or so. Our plan has been successful, but the occasion for getting together has not always been happy. There have been funerals as well as weddings. In addition, anniversaries and milestone birthdays have served to bring us together.

In happy times or times of grief there is joy and strength is found while sharing life with those with whom you have a shared history.

One of my favorite axioms is a Swedish proverb that declares, "A shared joy is a doubled joy and a shared sorrow is half a sorrow."

From my perspective as a man of the cloth, family reunions are a preview of coming attractions. They point to what awaits us on the other side. My understanding of Heaven is more than simply escaping the heartaches and hard times of this world. From what I read in the Bible, Heaven will also include a wonderful reunion with loved ones who have entered into the presence of the Lord ahead of us. Often while conducting graveside services at a local cemetery, I will remind the grieving that there is an ultimate family reunion that yet awaits. Such a reminder offers hope in the midst of sorrow.

Although death provides a doorway to that grand reunion to come, our faith entitles us to benefit from family reunions on this side of the sod. Since retiring from fulltime ministry a year ago, my wife and I have been attending a small church where I am not the pastor. As a matter of fact, our daughter's husband is one of the ministers. Attending that church allows us to support our son-in-law as well as model generational faith for our two granddaughters.

In the process of breaking into a new congregation, we have discovered friendship with others who attend Creekside Covenant Church. Every Sunday we look forward to seeing them. And they look forward to seeing us. We have become like extended family members to one another. As Wendy and I learn of health concerns that cause our new friends fear or high school graduations that cause them joy, we are able to "do life" with them. Shared joys and shared sorrows connect us.

All that to say, going to church on a Sunday morning has become like a weekly family reunion. We enjoy seeing people we care about and we feel loved by them at the same time.

Since COVID there has been a tendency for many to continue "doing church" virtually. We can stay in our sweats and drink coffee with our feet elevated in our recliners as the worship band plays and the pastor preaches. And while that may be convenient, it is not optimal. The family reunion feel of in-person church attendance is lost when we opt for online attendance.

No wonder the person who wrote the Epistle to the Hebrews chided the first century Christians to not forsake the practice of regular church attendance. *"Let us not give up meeting together, as some are in the habit of doing, but encourage one another—and all the more as you see the Day approaching."* (Hebrews 10:25)

A Puff Felt Round the World

This week marks the 75th anniversary of Billy Graham's first major evangelistic crusade. It was held in Los Angeles. On September 25, 1949, the thirty-year-old blond evangelist stood on a platform in a circus tent that accommodated a waiting crowd of six thousand. It was the first night of a planned three-week event. What began relatively slowly within a few weeks became a much talked-about happening.

Newspaper magnate William Randolf Hearst, sensing the magnitude of the moment, issued a two-word directive to his various news outlets. The message simply instructed his editors to "Puff Graham." The results of the telegram were mindboggling. The revival, at the corner of Washington and Hill streets, proved to be so popular, the crusade was extended five additional weeks and the tent was enlarged to seat 9,000. Billy Graham became an overnight phenomenon nationwide.

Before his storied career ended with his final crusade in New York in 2005, the North Carolina native had preached the Gospel to an estimated 250 million souls around the world. Graham would return to Los Angeles six more times following his initial "big tent revival" in 1949.

One of those return visits was in the summer of 1963. My neighbor and longtime friend, Linda Nicholl, remembers it well. Although she was in college at the time, she recalls reports from her folks. Linda's dad,

Dan Thrapp, was the religion editor for the Los Angeles Times for a quarter of a century. The Graham Crusades in the Southland were the heart of his beat whenever Billy came to town.

Recently Linda showed me the front page of the LA newspaper featuring her father's recap of the three-week crusade in Memorial Coliseum. As I studied that treasured bit of family history, I pieced together the events of that momentous year nationally.

The same summer that 250,000 gathered on the Washington Mall to hear Martin Luther King, Jr. deliver his "I Have a Dream" speech, nearly a million gathered at the site of the 1932 Olympic Games to hear Billy Graham proclaim God's dream for humanity. King and Graham, both Baptist ministers from the South, articulated a call to action. For MLK it was a call to peaceful protests. For Billy it was a call to protest sin and find peace with God by walking the aisle while the crusade choir sang "Just As I Am."

At the last night of his three-week campaign, the popular evangelist drew a crowd of more than 134,000. 20,000 additional would-be attendees, who were unable to get seats, listened over a sound system outside the stadium.

Ironically (and tragically) two weeks after King's speech and a week after Graham's final sermon, four little Black girls were killed when a bomb was detonated at the 16th Street Baptist Church in Birmingham, Alabama. Both ministers' dreams remained unrealized.

And just two months later Lee Harvey Oswald would gun down President John F. Kennedy in Dallas. The evidence of injustice, depravity and hatred replaced "good news" stories on the front pages of newspapers around the country. A nation hungry for words of hope and healing found themselves grieving and disenchanted.

Today, seventy-five years after William Randolph Hearst "puffed" Graham's message, I'm convinced the late evangelist's approach to getting the Word out would no longer draw huge crowds. It's a different day requiring different methods. But I'm also convinced that both MLK's dream and Billy's theme need a fresh hearing. As in 1963, greed and pride often trump compassion and hope.

Racial injustice, political division, Biblical illiteracy, corporate corruption, moral bankruptcy and mass shootings all point to a three-letter-word that Dr. Graham used often. For him sin was the root cause of humanity's ills. For Billy, sin was at the heart of people's hearts. Personally, I heard Billy Graham bare his soul at his Los Angeles Crusade in 1985. From his pulpit at second base in Angels Stadium, he pitched his invitation to acknowledge a need for God. Billy defined that three-letter word as the source of broken homes, broken marriages and a broken world. But he didn't stop with the definition. Billy's message included a solution. It was a four-letter word called LOVE.

The Passion (Revisited)

Where did you see Mel Gibson's epic drama "The Passion of the Christ?" I watched it with a few other pastors at Willow Creek Community Church in suburban Chicago. I will never forget being handed a package of Kleenex as we entered the auditorium that seats some 7,000 people. The free gift was in anticipation of the emotional impact the film documenting the final hours of Jesus life would have.

A year ago it dawned on me that the twentieth anniversary of the film's release was approaching. Wouldn't it be great if I could get an interview with Jim Caviezel who played the part of Jesus in Gibson's blockbuster hit? And so my passion this past year has been to find a way to contact the Hollywood actor raised just north of Seattle. I reached out to friends who knew his brother. No success. I enlisted the help of people with media connections. I emailed Jim's agent after a friend who produced one of Jim's earlier movies came through for me. But no response.

My passion to persist on my goal was ebbing when a business leader in our community emailed. Doris wanted to know if I'd like to have dinner with Jim Caviezel. She had no idea of my yearlong pursuit. Of course, I'd be delighted. And so my wife and I joined our dear friend for an evening I will long remember.

It didn't matter that dinner with Jim included over five hundred others who wanted to hear this gifted actor share his life story. I was grateful to discover this one who personified Christ in The Passion was passionate for living out the message of the one he portrayed in the film.

Standing under a light fixture that ironically boasted the shape of a cross, Jim admitted to the sacred privilege he felt to be cast as the Savior he faithfully worships as a devout Roman Catholic. With a wry smile he indicated that the reason Mel Gibson chose him for the part was more than the fact that his initials were J C and that he was thirty-three years old.

Jim described the incredible physical toll the crucifixion scene took on his body. What we witnessed in that realistic reenactment was not created by stunt doubles or special effects. Jim indicated he nearly lost his life from the intense suffering. He could not have anticipated what he signed up for.

But chronicling his role in The Passion was not the primary purpose of Jim's presentation. He also talked about his most recent film The Sound of Freedom that deals with freeing children from the sex trafficking industry in Latin America. As he described what was involved in playing the life of Tim Ballard, whose true story is documented in the movie, he waxed eloquent on the topic of freedom.

His desire is to awaken a sleeping culture to the trafficking that occurs not only south of our border and in Southeast Asia, but in our own country as well. He is committing himself to freeing innocent victims from a plight worse than death.

Jim is also concerned that we not take our personal freedoms for granted. He believes freedom must be courageously defended on the frontlines and in the public square. Employing his enviable impersonation of Ronald Reagan, Gibson's "Christ" passionately challenged me and the others in the crowd with the actor-turned-President's words from October 1964.

You and I know and do not believe that life is so dear and peace so sweet as to be purchased at the price of chains and slavery. If nothing in life is worth dying for, when did this begin - just in the face of this enemy? Or should Moses have told the children of Israel to live in slavery under the pharaohs? Should Christ have refused the cross? Should the patriots at Concord Bridge have thrown down their guns and refused to fire the shot heard 'round the world? The martyrs of history were not fools, and our honored dead who gave their lives to stop the advance of the Nazis didn't die in vain. Where, then, is the road to peace? Well, it's a simple answer after all.

Perspective is Everything

While in Lucerne, Switzerland earlier this year, I climbed a lookout tower on the six-hundred-year-old wall around the medieval portion of the city. From that vantage point I had an incredible view of Lake Lucerne, the Reuss River and the Swiss Alps in the distance. The perspective from my perch was breathtaking. And the photo I was able to capture on my iPhone provided me a memory of a moment I'll not soon forget. It was almost spiritual.

I had a similar experience a few weeks ago while spending time at our lake cottage in Chelan. While drifting off to sleep, I received a text informing me of the death of my best friend from childhood. That sobering news kept me awake for a while. And when I did drift off to sleep, I didn't sleep long. I woke up before sunrise. After a cup of coffee, I decided to take advantage of the early morning hour and find a spot to view the sunrise.

Driving to the new cemetery above town, I saw a spot where I could look down on the entire Chelan Valley. It was amazing. I thought, If I am able to see for miles from this lookout, then God has an even more complete view of our world. From His vantage point in Heaven, the Creator can picture what's going on in minute detail.

Not so for us. We question why loved ones die prematurely, why jobs are terminated without cause, why couples who long to be parents can't conceive, why unethical people succeed while those with integrity barely get by. So much of what puzzles us remains a mystery to us because of our limited perspective.

As I stood surveying the expansive scene before me, lyrics from an old Gospel hymn came to mind.

If we could see beyond today as God can see,
if all the clouds should roll away, the shadows flee,
o'er present griefs we would not fret,
each sorrow we would soon forget,
for many joys are waiting yet, for you and me.

Indeed. If only we could see as God sees, we'd be able to let go of those things and issues that cause us so much consternation. If only we could see the big picture.

As I continued looking down at the south shore of Lake Chelan, I noticed the neatly platted commercial district of the town. I saw Campbell's Resort and the Grand View hotel. I was even able to spot our family cottage in the distance. But I was also able to see (with the eyes of faith) something that brought comfort to my heart. I pictured Heaven's perspective of earth.

Because I was standing adjacent to the Chelan cemetery, I couldn't help but wonder what those who recently closed their eyes in death were able to see from where they are now. I thought back to the phone text I'd received a few hours before. I wondered what kind of view my buddy Billy was enjoying from his perch in the presence of the living God. His struggles in recent years due to Parkinson's disease are over. The debilitating symptoms that held him hostage have lost their grip on him. I could visualize Billy more alive than he ever was on earth drinking in nourishing refreshing taste of eternal life.

As the hymnwriter observed, present griefs need not fret us. Sorrows that blindside us can be overlooked. And all because of the joys that await those who have discovered the means to see beyond today.

I waited on that hilltop overlooking Chelan until the sun crept over the horizon beyond the Columbia River. The first rays of a new day bathed the brown hills with a yellow-orange blanket. What I witnessed warmed my heart with a fresh understanding of how God's bird's eye view differs from mine. Yes, perspective is everything.

Welcome to Awe-tumn

"I just love this time of year!" My wife Wendy verbalized what I was thinking as she pulled open the shades and looked into our backyard. The morning light was illuminating the park-like view we enjoy from our family room. The Japanese vine maple trees were boasting their colors while their leaves began to carpet our patio.

It's amazing. Every fall we tend to fall into a trance. The crisp cold nights and warm sunny afternoons have a way of holding our hearts hostage. And we aren't in a hurry to be set free. Wendy enjoys brewing hot cider in our old coffee percolator. Our grandkids love visiting the local pumpkin patch. And I find great joy walking through the nearby forest gazing at the Kodachrome wonderland of color.

Years ago, *The New Yorker* magazine featured a cover that caught my attention. I loved it so much, I saved it. It's a whimsical scene of the Creator reaching down from Heaven touching the trees and transforming their green leaves into red, orange and yellow.

Upon closer examination, you discover that the Almighty is not alone. He is surrounded by cherubs who are aiming their cameras taking photos of the phenomenon. What I like is the fact that the beauty of this time of year is attributed to the One we worship as the giver and sustainer of life.

Autumn is definitely a photo-op. The pictures on my iPhone bear witness to that. But autumn is much more. The fall season is a time for reflection. It is an opportunity to contemplate the spiritual dimension of our lives. It's a chance to ask ourselves why we are awed by the beauty of fall colors. What (or Who) accounts for our emotional response to all things beautiful? As the leaves fall, why not look up?

Sometime back I penned these words in my journal: *"Autumn leaves us awed with wonder. Trees once green blush red and gold. Darkness draws its early curtain. Balmy nights turn frosty cold. Mystery abounds in nature. In this season God we see."*

Autumn is that shoulder season between summer and winter when we are reminded of the fleeting nature of life and the inevitability of death. Flowers lose their bloom. Trees lose their leaves. The hours of daylight disappear before our very eyes. Fall is an annual metaphor for what awaits each one of us.

The Hebrew prophet Isaiah observed the inescapable destiny of plant life and human life when he observed that *"the grass withers and the flower fades…"* (Isaiah 40:8) The psalmist journaled essentially the same thought when he wrote *"My days are like a lengthened shadow, and I wither away like grass."* (Psalm 102:11)

A morbid thought? Not necessarily. The same Bible that declares the universality of death, also says this: *Precious in the sight of the Lord is the death of His saints."* (Psalm 116:15) And by saints he means people who belong to Him. Even King Solomon was credited with saying, *"The day of our death is better than the day of our birth."* (Ecclesiastes 7:1). Death is not to be feared. There is glory in the mystery of passing beyond the veil of this life. Death is a thing of beauty for those whose faith provides them the assurance of eternal life.

And speaking of death, get this: The fall leaves we delight in and love to photograph are incredibly beautiful because they have ceased to live or are in the process of dying. In autumn, the Master Artist has given us a visual aid of a timeless principle. Though it often comes with darkness, drizzle, wind and cold, in death there is glory. In death, like in the fall season, there is cause for awe.

At the start of each of the four seasons and for milestone holidays, we decorate our fireplace mantel with large wooden blocks. The blocks call attention to what's happening in our family or in the world. This week we are celebrating autumn. But as you might expect we spell autumn a bit differently than most. We spell it AWE-TUMN.

Fully Rely on God

I've been reflecting on the wonderful life of a local Wenatchee businessman who died earlier this summer at the age of ninety-seven. Earl Carey, like George Bailey in the movie "It's a Wonderful Life," was a smalltown hero to those who knew him. Over the years the "Earl of Wenatchee" owned the local bus line, a taxi cab company and an ambulance service. But Earl was best known for his years spent with the United States Postal Service. With that in mind, I think you could say that Earl Carey was "a man of letters."

I first met Earl in 1964 when he moved his family to Wenatchee from Hartline. That was the same year our family moved to the Valley from Marysville. At that time both his family and our family attended First Assembly of God Church. Earl was our regular song leader for worship services on Sunday mornings. His style of leading the hymns was unique and notable. Instead of waving his hand to signify the time signature of the song, he would punch the air with his closed-finger right hand to indicate if the notes went up or down.

Earl would lead us in well-known hymns like "All Hail the Power of Jesus' Name," Great is Thy Faithfulness" and "Amazing Grace." Decades before Earl's grandson Josh McPherson would become the lead pastor of a Wenatchee church called "Grace City," I was learning from his Grandpa Earl the essence of what God's grace was about. As Brother Carey led us in singing Amazing Grace, I was being bathed in an awareness of my identity in Christ.

Although not nearly as theologically profound John Newton's lyrics, I learned an acrostic for GRACE as I continued to prepare for my career as a pastor after graduating from Seattle Pacific University. **God's Riches At Christ's Expense.** Those five words whose first initials spell out GRACE convey the basic Christian doctrine that we do not earn God's favor through our good works.

There was another acrostic I learned later in life from my little mother. Always the life of the party, my mom loved to entertain others with riddles and clever sayings. One of her favorites was Q: "What did one eye say to the other eye?" A: "There's something between us that smells." Another was "Age is just a number and mine's unlisted."

But my mom also would ask friends and strangers alike the following: "Do you know how to spell FROG?" And before they could respond, she would answer with a smile on her face. **F**ully **R**ely **O**n **G**od.

As I pondered my mom's acrostic for FROG, it occurred to me that she was illustrating the essence of GRACE. Since we cannot obligate the Almighty with our attempts at being righteous, we can only acknowledge our need of a Savior by fully relying on Him to save us. Believe it or not, I have used my mom's saying in my ministry over and over again.

Even though my mom passed away five years ago, I think of her whenever I come across frog figurines that she collected displayed in our lake house in Chelan. And speaking of frog figurines, some months ago I was going through a pile of memorabilia I've saved from high school days. What caught my eye was a large green ceramic frog sitting on his haunches with one leg supporting his chin. This whimsical amphibian resembled Rodin's "the thinker" I saw earlier this year in a Paris museum. I knew there was a reason I had saved this frog.

But for the life of me I couldn't remember who had given it to me. And then I turned it over. To my surprise there was a name and a date that had been scratched into the bottom. The frog that has followed me around since 1970 was made and given to me by Candy Carey, Earl's daughter and Josh McPherson's mom. Candy had graced me with this unique gift the year I graduated from Wenatchee High School. To this day, it serves as a memory of her amazing father and one of my favorite hymns.

A Life-Saving Rescue Remembered

For ten years of my pastoral career, I was a chaplain in a faith-based retirement community. One of the joys of my job was being exposed to the fascinating life stories of the senior adults with whom I interacted. Among many others, the campus on which I served boasted a retired CIA agent, a former NFL coach, decorated military hero and a world-renown missionary.

One of the residents to which I was drawn was the granddaughter of the territorial governor of Alaska. As Ellie told me about her grandfather's contribution to Alaska history, I was touched by a real-life illustration of a powerful Gospel truth.

In January 1925 the lives of countless children in Nome, Alaska were at stake. A diphtheria outbreak threatened the entire town. Even though the situation was not as widespread as the coronavirus, fear reared its ugly head. Because Nome did not have a sufficient amount of the needed antitoxin, widespread death loomed. Dr. Curtis Welch, the local physician, telegraphed for help. The only supply of the life-saving serum was in Anchorage.

But there was a major obstacle to be overcome. How would the needed medicine be transported to Nome to stave off the epidemic? Since the Bering Sea was frozen and there were no railroad tracks or roads that led to Nome, dog teams were the only solution. Alaska's Governor

Scott Bone, who had been appointed by President Warren Harding, authorized the time-sensitive operation.

The units of serum were packed in a cylinder and wrapped in fur and canvas. The precious cargo was then transported from Anchorage to Nenana on an overnight train. From there the antitoxin was transported 674 miles by a sled dog relay in a race against time. It would ordinarily take a dog team and its musher a month to travel from Nenana to Nome. But the dying children needed the medicine much sooner than that.

Reading the history of the action that followed Governor Bone's decision, I learned that the first musher took the insulated cylinder fifty-two miles and passed it on to the second musher who traveled thirty-one miles. From musher to musher the relay continued involving a score of sled dog drivers and their teams. The needed medicine arrived in Nome just one-hundred-twenty-seven hours after the life-saving mission began. Nome's children were saved. Thanks to Governor Bone and a series of mushers and their teams, Doctor Welch received that for which he'd prayed.

The musher who had the privilege of reaching Nome with his team and the antitoxin was Leonhard Seppala. His lead dog was a Husky by the name of Balto. To commemorate this amazing true story of salvation, a statue of Seppala's best friend stands in Central Park in New York City. An animated movie named for this celebrated canine has also been produced.

As I contemplated this life-saving rescue that took place a hundred years ago, I couldn't help but think of another rescue that saved countless lives. Like the diphtheria epidemic in Nome, a life-threatening sickness plagued humanity. Much more grave than the pandemic of 2020, the virus of human depravity could not be eradicated by face masks and sheltering in place. Lockdowns and repeated testing would not offer more promising results. The infection of sin was universal and contagious. No one was exempt. And according to Romans 6:23, the wages of sin is death.

The only solution that would alter the deadly diagnosis was a blood transfusion provided by a sinless human. Like the relay team of mushers that carried the life-saving serum to Nome, a team of lawgivers, kings, prophets and angels transported the truth of God's remedy across the centuries. For more than two thousand years the message of a promised hope that would save humankind was carried forward. And now, two thousand years later, those who receive the offered transfusion avoid eternal death.

The Apostle Paul eloquently describes the lifesaving rescue that culminated in the cross. In the first chapter of Colossians, he describes the fulfillment of the relay-race of redemption that resulted in Jesus shedding his blood on our behalf. *For he has rescued us from the dominion of darkness and brought us into the kingdom of the Son he loves,* [14] *in whom we have redemption, the forgiveness of sins.*

This is Holy Ground

This past Wednesday our nation paused to catch its corporate breath. And in the pausing, we took time to remember a Tuesday we will never forget. The events of September 11, 2001 are forever seared into the membranes of our memories. Two towers. Four planes and nearly 3,000 victims. At Ground Zero the names of those who perished are read by family members every year in a solemn remembrance ceremony.

A week ago while driving back home from Lake Chelan, I stopped at the 9/11 Spirit of America Memorial in Cashmere. Once again, I was touched by what I witnessed. The sculpture representing the first responders is deeply moving. So is the miniature replica of the twin towers with the names of the fallen engraved on each. The pieces of rubble from Ground Zero and the memorials to the crash sites at the Pentagon and Shanksville call to mind our national grief.

I continue to be amazed by the number of people I meet on both sides of the Cascades who have not visited the Cashmere memorial. It is a garden of remembrance disproportional to the size of the community in which it is housed. In my opinion it is holy ground.

As a clergyman in the Seattle area for the past two decades, I have conducted memorial services at Tahoma National Cemetery in Covington on a regular basis. The two most memorable occasions were the internment of President Nixon's brother and the great-grandson of the man who wrote the timeless hymn "It is Well with My Soul." And although those occasions were special, every time I drive through the gates of Tahoma, I feel I am entering sacred space. The sign at the entrance to Tahoma is noteworthy. It announces "Where Heroes Rest."

The 9/11 Memorial in Cashmere leaves me with the same feeling as trips to Tahoma. Although there are no remains interred at the Spirit of America in Cashmere, the site is sacred space. Like a cemetery, it triggers the grave awareness that life is brief, death is sure and we must be prepared.

Three years ago, I had the privilege of chauffeuring the parents of Todd Beamer, one of the passengers on doomed Flight 93, to the Memorial. David and Peggy Beamer were the guests of honor for the twentieth anniversary commemoration of 9/11. I recall how deeply moved the Beamers were when they arrived at the Cashmere location.

As he stood to offer his keynote address, David Beamer reminded his audience of the details of the day that blindsided our democracy. Listening to David, it was obvious that none of those who perished that fateful Tuesday had any idea it would be their last day of life. His son Todd had just returned the previous night from a European vacation with his pregnant wife. Those who officed in the towers of the World Trade Center thought they were simply putting in a routine day of work. The firefighters who responded to Ground Zero didn't realize how the day would end.

Because of David and Peggy Beamer's contribution to the Spirit of America Memorial three years ago, I will often text them a photo from the plaque in Cashmere that honors their son and the others on Flight 93.

While the Spirit of America Memorial invites us to ponder the price tag associated with our freedoms as a nation, it calls to mind much more. It is a beautifully maintained rest stop on our life's journey where we are where we can't help but contemplate the reality of our own death.

Like other rest stops, this Cashmere location allows us the opportunity to take a break from the speed at which we are barreling down life's highway to pause and stretch our legs, catch our breath and listen to our hearts. What is more, the Spirit of America Memorial actually is a rest stop complete with a nearby playground, a grassy field and restrooms.

But mostly, it is a rest stop that provides those who take the time to press the pause button a reboot of our perspective. If you've never visited this nearby treasure, do so soon.

A Tale of Three Amigos

In the New Testament there is an account of the Apostle Paul going on a mission trip with his colleague by the name of Joseph. If you're familiar with the New Testament and that name doesn't sound familiar, there's good reason. It's because Joseph went by a nickname. He was called "Barnabas" which in Hebrew meant "son of encouragement."

Joseph was definitely that. His encouragement was seen in his desire to have his young cousin tag along on the trip. John Mark was grateful for the opportunity but (as the Scriptures indicate) was prone to homesickness. As it turned out, young John Mark ended up bailing out on Paul and Barnabas. It wasn't a happy scene. But his caring cousin continued to advocate for him when Paul planned their next trip.

When you feel all alone and on your own, you need a Barnabas. I sure did! In fact, I needed two "sons of encouragement." Nineteen years ago, our family moved from the Midwest to Mercer Island. I was excited about my new call to be lead pastor at the local Covenant church. But I was also feeling homesick for a town in the suburbs of Chicago our family dearly loved.

As we were settling into life on Mercer Island, two individuals sought me out and introduced themselves to me. Dale Sewall was the senior minister at the local Presbyterian church and Paul Fauske was the pastor of the local Lutheran church. As longtime leaders in our community, they were much in demand. Their schedules were full. But they made time for me.

Over coffee at St. Arbucks they reflected on what it was like when they moved to Mercer Island. They took the time to introduce me to other people of influence in town. They drew me in and treated me like their little brother.

As I contemplate what these two colleagues did for me as I began my ministry in our community, I see a universal Biblical principle at play. In the creation story as recorded in Genesis we find the Creator going on record to say it is not good for the human he created to be alone. And so the Almighty created a companion with whom the man could share life. That was the first indication that isolated lives are detrimental to God's intention for humanity.

By the time we get to the New Testament we discover the principle of community is a cherished value. There is a rabbi named Jesus who identifies a dozen disciples with whom to spend time and in whom to invest his teachings. What is more Jesus surrounds himself with an inner circle of three close friends. And when this popular rabbi sends out his disciples to meet the physical and spiritual needs of those in various villages, he sends them out two-by-two.

I'm guessing Jesus took his cue from wise King Solomon who lived a thousand years before a three wisemen from the East (or however many there were) traveled to Bethlehem with gold, frankincense and myrrh to celebrate his birth.

In one of my favorite Biblical passages dealing with companionship, Solomon wrote, *"Two are better than one, because they have a good return for their labor: If either of them falls down, one can help the other up. But pity anyone who falls and has no one to help them up. But pity anyone who falls and has no one to help them up. Also, if two lie down together, they will keep warm. But how can one keep warm alone? Though one may be overpowered, two can defend themselves. A cord of three strands is not quickly broken."* (Ecclesiastes 4:9-12)

A Scandinavian proverb celebrates a similar theme: *"A shared joy is a doubled joy; a shared sorrow is half a sorrow."*

Although Paul Fauske, Dale Sewall and I have all retired from active ministry, there is a bond of friendship that remains. We celebrated that bond not long ago over Mexican food in Factoria. As we dipped our tortilla chips into the common bowl of salsa, I couldn't help but smile. Their gift of encouragement nineteen years ago is a gift that keeps on giving.

Your House versus the White House

Am I the only one who approaches this month of giving thanks grateful that the campaign season is over? I'm guessing not. The multitude of ads has been maddening. The content of the candidates' commercials has been controversial. The name calling and character attacks has been juvenile. Regardless of what network you choose for your daily diet of news, what's been served up the past several months has been anything but nourishing. In spite of the outcome of this week's election, our United States of America will be anything but.

I am reminded of the words of a first century carpenter-turned-rabbi who said, *"A house divided against itself cannot stand."* Although Abraham Lincoln used that famous line in one of his memorable campaign speeches, it was Jesus of Nazareth who coined the expression. What is true for a family or a congregation of the faithful is also true for a nation. A nation divided is terminally ill.

As I reflect on Jesus' teaching and values, I'm convinced that the antidote to alienation is understanding, forgiveness and compassion. Divisions are healed as we love our neighbors to the degree we love ourselves and to the degree we treat them the way we desire to be treated. How we engage or distance ourselves from those who see life differently than we do has lasting ramifications. Our ongoing attitude and actions toward our political rivals will impact us as well as them. Active animosity can poison the well of friendship within a family, in a faith community or in a work environment.

In her bestselling book "A Team of Rivals" presidential biographer Doris Kearns Goodwin chronicles how Abraham Lincoln chose men who had run against him in his 1860 campaign to serve in his cabinet. The book focuses on our sixteenth president's mostly successful attempts to reconcile conflicting personalities and political factions on the path to abolition and victory in the American Civil War.

Acknowledging conflict and conflicting views rather than ignoring them, Lincoln proactively engaged the divisions and challenges he faced. He recognized to what degree cooperation depended on him and then made choices accordingly. Our country's most popular president was no doubt familiar what Saint Paul wrote to the first century Christians in Rome: *If it is possible, as far as it depends on you, live at peace with everyone.* (Romans 12:18)

As a man of the cloth who resists addressing political issues from the pulpit, I have come to the conclusion that the results of this year's election will not thwart the sovereign plan of the Almighty. And in the broad scheme of human history, the individual the Electoral College will select will not matter as much as we might think. A look back at presidents over nearly two-hundred-and-fifty years will bear that out.

Granted, the person who will inhabit the White House for the next four years may or may not be the person whose candidacy you supported. The fact that they will lead from that residence is obviously significant. That person will influence the future direction of our republic. Their personal values and worldview will determine what is prioritized and what is put on the back burner.

All the same it is my personal belief that the person who is about to move into the White House matters less than the individuals who currently live in your house. Our nation's future ultimately depends on the character qualities being shaped and practiced by you and your family in your neighborhood and in your community. Who you are, how you think, what you say, how you act and how you react will have a far more lasting impact on our nation than the temporary inhabitants of 1600 Pennsylvania Avenue.

You matter more than you may think. As we have been reminded in recent weeks, your vote matters. It is your voice in a democratic republic. But even after all the votes have been tabulated, the fabric of your friendship, faith and compassion is what clothes the future of the nation we love regardless of who is our president.

Preparing for the Trip of a Lifetime

For the past ten years I was the chaplain at a continuing care retirement community. Among other tasks, the most meaningful part of my job was making sure those who were approaching the end of their earthly journey were ready for the journey to come. I referred to this sacred calling as helping the residents "pack their bags for heaven."

Having recently retired, I am mindful that my own trip of a lifetime is closer than ever before. As a result, the advice I gave to the residents is the same advice I'd do well to heed.

Reviewing the itinerary. It is important to spend time reading about and thinking about where we're headed. Just as my wife and I watch YouTubes and browse travel brochures about places we are planning to visit, so too, we would do well to focus our thoughts on heaven. Reading passages of Scriptures and books that focus on our future destination whets our appetite for what's to come. Listening to worship music about Heaven inspires our faith.

Securing house before leaving. Whenever my wife and I leave on a trip, we do a final check with a walk-through of our home. We verify that the appliances are unplugged, the windows are closed and the deadbolt lock on the front door is secured. Such a security check allows us peace of mind as we leave on our adventure. With regard to the trip that awaits us when we leave our earthly home, it is important that we have done a security check of our readiness to leave. Such a checklist involves reviewing the assurance of our salvation. Being able to verbalize our confidence that we have accepted God's offer of eternal life by appropriating Christ's death and resurrection provides us that blessed assurance.

<u>Calling neighbors</u>. When Wendy and I take off for some time away, we will often alert our neighbors that we will be gone. That way they can be aware of any suspicious activity around our home while we are away. If we are expecting a package to be delivered, we might ask the couple next door to pick it up so it won't be stolen. When it comes to preparing for a trip that's out of this world, there is another kind of call that makes sense. It's a call to (or a face-to-face visit with) to those with whom we want to say goodbye. A chance to say so-long allows closure for the person dying as well as those who are left behind. And if there have been relational difficulties, that contact gives the chance to ask for forgiveness or to extend forgiveness.

<u>Leaving a letter for loved ones</u>. Since I was a young pastor, whenever I would leave home for a ministry conference or a speaking assignment, I would leave my wife and my kids a note relating how much I loved them and how much I would miss them. I would use that written expression as an opportunity to remind them of what needed to be done while I was gone. Similarly, as we prepare to take off for our Father's house, it is incumbent on us to communicate how much we love our family and how much we want to spend eternity with them. Spelling out the simple plan of salvation in words they can understand is most appropriate. Another important communique to leave behind should include instructions on what you would like your memorial service to include. Be clear as to who you'd like to speak, what Scriptures you'd like read, what songs you'd like sung and how much you look forward to seeing them again.

<u>Remember your keys</u>. The old television commercial for the American Express card reminded us to "not leave home without it." It was more than a catchy slogan. It was a helpful reminder to not forget what's essential. Apart from a credit card, the most important thing I've learned not to forget as I leave on a trip is my house key. And when it

comes to the most important trip we will ever take, that key truly is the key. I'm referring to the cross. When my dad died fifteen years ago, he was clutching a little wooden cross. He clung to that handmade cross for the last weeks of his life. Ever since that memorable day, I have shared a similar holding cross with those I care about who are nearing the end. It's a simple visual aid that calls to mind the key to our faith. And I have a cross for the day I leave for home.

Faith Matters! It Really Does

Snoqualmie Falls is one of the most popular tourist attractions in the State of Washington. It is, in fact, the second most visited site next to Mount Rainier. At 268 feet, it is almost one hundred feet taller than Niagara Falls. Experiencing the mist and the roar of the cascading water from the viewpoint is powerful. I never tire of introducing out-of-town guests to the breathtaking beauty of this natural landmark.

Whereas Snoqualmie Falls is surprisingly higher than Niagara Falls, the latter is significantly wider. At 2,200 feet it is an impressive vista to behold. And the thought of traversing the width of the falls is almost inconceivable. But you probably remember when Nick Wallenda, of the Flying Wallenda family, achieved this death-defying feat in 2012. But he wasn't the first.

Have you ever heard of Charles Blondin? In 1859, this French acrobat walked on a tightrope 160 feet above Niagara Falls several times back and forth between Canada and the United States. As huge crowds looked on, Blondin dazzled them with dramatic dare-devil exploits. He crossed blindfolded, once on stilts, another time on a bicycle and once he even carried a stove and cooked an omelet!

As legend has it, Blondin asked the growing gallery of gawkers if they believed he could push a wheelbarrow across the chasm on the highwire. When the crowd enthusiastically confessed their belief, the fearless performer said, "If you believe, are you willing to get in the wheelbarrow?"

Gulp! Ever since I was a young man contemplating a career as a pastor, I've heard that illustration repeated time and again. Although a bit hyperbolic, it attempts to describe the difference between belief and faith. Whereas belief attests to the possibility of a given outcome, faith rests it weight in the process. I can say I believe a chair will hold me up. However, I translate my belief into faith by actually sitting in the chair.

Believing is relatively risk-free. We can say we believe most anything. But faith comes with a cost. Faith demands you act on what you claim to be true. As such, faith can be life-altering.

For Christians around the world, this is the season on the liturgical calendar known as Lent. It is that period of six weeks set aside for personal introspection. Followers of Jesus are invited to reflect on his invitation: *"If anyone would be my disciple, let him deny himself and take up his cross and follow me."*

Lent is an opportunity to differentiate between mental assent to theological affirmations and putting into practice personal convictions that influence our behavior.

The journey of Lent is often associated with fasting from something central to our daily routine. It can mean giving up caffeine or alcohol or chocolate. Some friends of mine choose to fast from Facebook. Others choose to incorporate something new into their lives as a means of drawing nearer to God.

Such spiritual disciplines might include reading through the entire New Testament, doing a weekly prayer walk or keeping a gratitude journal. It could also involve volunteering at a neighborhood food kitchen, distributing socks in a homeless encampment or visiting shut-ins in an adult family home or care center.

As you might surmise, I'm grateful for this season of the year. Like Snoqualmie Falls, Lent provides a bird's-eye perspective. It gives us a vantage point of the churning white-capped world in which we attempt to find our faith-footing and balance our lives.

About the Author

Greg Asimakoupoulos has been called America's pastor/poet laureate. Over the past forty-five years, he has served congregations in California, Illinois and Washington State. Greg is the author of seventeen books and more than three hundred magazine articles. He writes a weekly newspaper column on faith and values as well as a weekly online blog that can be found at myrhymesandreasons.com

Greg and his wife Wendy have three grown daughters and two granddaughters and live in suburban Seattle.

About the Artist

J. Craig Thorpe is a NW artist, and former Presbyterian minister, specializing in landscape and railway themes. He studied industrial design in Pittsburgh PA and became fascinated by art and railroads with their unexpected connection to society's common good. Thorpe's recent book, Railroads, Art and American Life: an Artist's Memoir (Indiana University Press 2023), offers a unique vision for national mobility and civil society.

www.ingramcontent.com/pod-product-compliance
Lightning Source LLC
Chambersburg PA
CBHW022104150426
43195CB00008B/258